Building the Mosquito Fleet

The U.S. Navy's First Torpedo Boats

The Narragansett Bay excursion steamer Mount Hope *and the* Porter *at Newport, Rhode Island. (Courtesy Rhode Island Historical Society.)*

BUILDING THE MOSQUITO FLEET

THE U.S. NAVY'S FIRST TORPEDO BOATS

Richard V. Simpson

ARCADIA PUBLISHING

ISBN 978-0-7385-0508-4

Published by Arcadia Publishing
Charleston, South Carolina

Printed in the United States of America

Library of Congress Number: applied for.

For all general information contact Arcadia Publishing at:
Telephone 843-853-2070
Fax 843-853-0044
E-Mail sales@arcadiapublishing.com
For customer service and orders:
Toll-Free 1-888-313-2665

Visit us on the Internet at www.arcadiapublishing.com

The only known illustration of the Stiletto *rigged to use sails.*

Contents

Acknowledgments

Grateful appreciation goes to the many respondents who provided information on the history and developments chronicled in these pages. It is a pleasure to acknowledge several former colleagues at the Naval Undersea Warfare Center in Newport for helping while the manuscript progressed over a period of 20 years: Mary N. Barravecchia, head of the Newport Technical Library; William J. Conforti, senior editor of the Technical Information Division; and Arthur E. Burke, historian, retired from the Weapons Systems Department. Special thanks go to Lionel D. Wyld, Ph.D., who reviewed the completed text and provided many valuable suggestions to help make this effort an accurate, readable, and well-organized record. I am indebted to Will Willoughby at Arcadia Publishing for designing and editing this book.

Note on illustrations: The photographs and illustrations in this book are from diverse sources, and every effort has been made to identify those sources: contemporary periodicals, artists' representations, picture postcard reproductions, U.S. Navy records, and other publications in the public domain. Generally, unattributed illustrations are from U.S. government archives that have been released for publication.

Bibliography

In addition to specific works cited below, material of relevance to the subject of this book can be found in the Providence (Rhode Island) Public Library, the Rhode Island Historical Society archives (extensive newspaper clippings collection by subject from the *Providence Journal* and other local newspapers), at the Naval War College Archives (papers on the history of the Naval Torpedo Station at Newport), and in various technical documents issued by the former Naval Underwater Systems Center (NUSC), one of the successor establishments of the original Naval Torpedo Station at Newport.

Abbot, Willis J. *Blue Jackets of 1898.* New York: Dodd, Mead & Company, 1899.

Armstrong, G.E. *Torpedoes & Torpedo-Vessels,* Royal Navy handbook. George Bell and Sons, 1889.

Bray, Maynard and Carlton S. Pinheiro. *Herreshoff of Bristol*. Brooklin, Maine: Woodenboat Publications, 1989.

Bristol, Rhode Island Celebration Committee. *Bristol: Three Hundred Years.* Providence: Franklin Graphics, 1980.

Burnett, Constance Bull. *Let the Best Boat Win.* Boston: Houghton Mifflin Company, 1957.

Carter, Samuel III. *The Boatbuilders of Bristol.* Garden City, New York: Doubleday & Company, 1970.

Coggeshall, W.J. and J.E. McCarthy. *The Naval Torpedo Station, Newport, Rhode Island.* Newport, Rhode Island: Remington Ward, 1944.

Daniels, Josephus. *The First Fallen Hero.* Norfolk, Virginia: Sam W. Bowman, 1898.

Dictionary of American Naval Fighting Ships. Washington, D.C.: U.S. Government Printing Office, 1969.

Friedman, Norman. *US. Destroyers: An Illustrated History.* Annapolis, Maryland: Naval Institute Press, 1982.

———. *US Small Combatants.* Annapolis, Maryland: Naval Institute Press, 1987.

Herreshoff, L. Francis. *Captain Nat Herreshoff: The Wizard of Bristol.* New York: Sheridan House, 1953.

Harper's New Monthly Magazine, "Torpedoes and Torpedo Boats," pp. 36–46, Vol. LXV, June–November 1882.

Jane, Fred T. *The Torpedo in Peace and War.* London: W Thacker & Company, 1898.

Navy Yearbook, Compilation of Annual Naval Appropriation Laws from 1883 to 1913. U.S. Government Printing Office.

Pinheiro, Carlton S. "The Herreshoff Manufacturing Company. A Remarkable Yankee Enterprise, Part I: The Early Years of the Dynasty." *Old Rhode Island,* Vol. 3, Issue 6.

———. "Part III: The Depression, A Hurricane & World War II." *Old Rhode Island,* Vol. 3, Issue 8, 1993.

Rhode Island: A Guide to the Smallest State. Federal Workers Project. Boston: Houghton Mifflin Company, 1937.

Rhode Island in the War with Spain. Compiled from the official records of the Executive Department of the State of Rhode Island and Providence Plantations, Providence: E.L. Freeman & Sons, 1900.

Shafer, Richard A. *Destroyers in Action*. New York: Cornell Maritime Press, 1945.

Sleeman, C.W. *Torpedoes and Torpedo Warfare.* Portsmouth, England: Simpkin, Marshall & Company, 1880.

Society of Naval Architects and Marine Engineers. *Transactions.* Washington, D.C.: Gibson Brothers. Vol. V, 1897.

Spears, John R. *Our Navy in the War with Spain.* New York: Charles Scribners Sons, 1898.

"The Swift *Stiletto.*" *Frank Leslie Illustrated Newspaper.* No. 1, 552, Vol. LX, NY, June 20, 1885.

Titherington, Richard H. "Our War with Spain," *Munsey's Magazine*, Vol. XX, October 1898–March 1899.

"Uncle Sam's Navy." Historical Fine Art Series. Vol. IV, No. 9. Philadelphia: Historical Publishing Company, May 31, 1898.

Young, James Rankin. *War with Spain.* Privately printed, 1898.

———. *Reminiscences and Thrilling Stories of the War.* Philadelphia: J.H. Moore Company, 1899.

Preface

In 1877, the U.S. Navy purchased a fast steam yacht built by the Herreshoff Manufacturing Company of Bristol, Rhode Island, for "submarine" torpedo experiments in Narragansett Bay. The boat—the USS *Stiletto* (Wooden Torpedo Boat No. 1)—was assigned for the next 24 years to the Naval Torpedo Station (NTS) at Newport, on Goat Island. Torpedo experiments were conducted by civilian engineers and technicians from the navy's torpedo experimentation and manufacturing facility. Dating from the Civil War period, the NTS on Goat Island was the first torpedo factory of its kind in the United States; it is the predecessor of today's Naval Undersea Warfare Center (NUWC), Newport Division.

This book traces the history of the involvement between the navy and the Herreshoff brothers' marine yards in Bristol, Rhode Island, over a period of 30 or more years. It is a story of enterprise, naval development, and marine manufacturing during a time of experimentation, evaluation, and evolution. The submarine service was in its infancy, and interest in the torpedo as an undersea weapon flourished. This group of vessels evolved into what was dubbed the mosquito fleet. Herreshoff's fast steam-powered boats were the first of the delivery platforms accepted by the navy for both experimental and service use.

Building the Mosquito Fleet: The U.S. Navy's First Torpedo Boats is an attempt to preserve under one cover a brief history of the torpedo boats built by the Herreshoff Manufacturing Company. It describes design and construction innovations introduced by the Herreshoffs and traces the events that led the major navies of the world to take notice of the Herreshoffs' work. This book also includes a complete listing and brief descriptions of all the navy torpedo boats built by the Herreshoff Manufacturing Company, along with a condensed service history of each vessel.

One
Beginnings

When boat lover John Brown Herreshoff accepted a commission to design and build a yacht for Thomas Clapham, he began an industry that thrived beyond all expectations and brought international fame to himself and to Bristol, Rhode Island. Herreshoff, blind at the age of 18, had acquired such a knowledge and feel of boats in his early years that his blindness was no obstacle. The handwork was done by his brother Nathanael Greene Herreshoff, known as "the Wizard of Bristol."

John Herreshoff had an exceptional memory and a photographic mind. His design method was to dictate specifications to his brother, who would then construct a model. By feeling this model, Herreshoff could find defects and suggest improvements with uncanny intuition.

The Herreshoff Manufacturing Company, located at Hope and Burnside Streets in Bristol, was established in 1863. Although the name Herreshoff has come to connote a long list of successful America's Cup defenders (dating back to the *Vigilant* in 1893),[1] this boatyard also designed and built hundreds of pleasure craft and service vessels.

In 1863, John Herreshoff, then only 22 years old, hired a crew of men, procured supplies of seasoned lumber, and fitted out an old tannery as a shop. The following year, nine sailing craft—ranging in length from 22 to 35 feet—were launched. As the business grew, an additional building on Burnside Street (the old Burnside Rifle Factory) was bought and converted to a sawmill for producing the enterprise's lumber.

By 1868, the Herreshoff Manufacturing Company had built its first steamer, the *Annie Morse,* followed in 1870 by the *Seven Brothers,* a pioneer fishing steamer built for the Church brothers of Tiverton, Rhode Island. As knowledge of the Herreshoff brothers' revolutionary steam engines spread, the company began receiving orders from several foreign governments for "submarine" torpedo boats; these became the first torpedo boats built in the United States.

Representing a new type of warship, the armored spar torpedo boat was first built for the British navy in 1878. The following excerpt from *Torpedoes and Torpedo Warfare,* a British pamphlet published in 1880, evaluates the Herreshoff Manufacturing Company's torpedo boats and steam engines:

> Messrs. Herreshoff, of Rhode Island, USA, have also constructed several torpedo boats. One of these was built for the English government. This boat is 59 feet 6 inches long, 7 feet 6 inches beam, and draws about 1 foot 3 inches of water. The vessel is constructed with five watertight bulkheads, and her hull is of composite construction below the water line, having a steel framing covered with wood planking. The upper part of the hull is wholly steel, the plates being 1/16 inch thick, the top sides sloping inwards and the upper work forming a protective superstructure

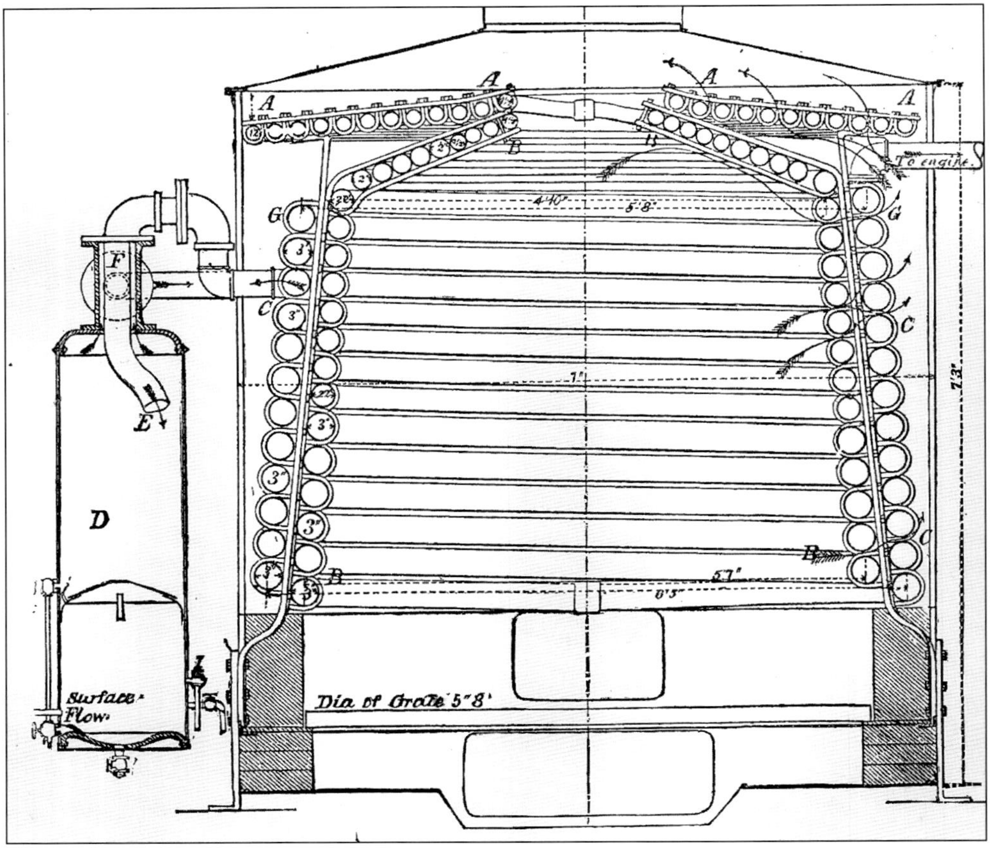

A Herreshoff steam generator. (Courtesy Scientific American.*)*

for crew and machinery. She is propelled by a screw that is placed beneath the vessel in a central position, and which is driven by a direct acting condensing engine placed in the forward part of the boat. The vessel is steered by means of a balanced rudder placed a short distance from the stern and under the ship, the helmsman being located in a stern cabin with a protected look-out raised just above the deck. The hull and machinery together weigh 6 tons, but with working crew of four men and fuel, stores, and two torpedoes on board, the boat weighs about 7.5 tons.

This vessel is guaranteed for a speed of 16 knots per hour. She can be propelled ahead or astern with equal speed, and can be brought to a dead stop when going full speed within a distance equal to her length.

Her turning powers are equally good. Her armament will probably be the Fish Torpedo.

In the late 1870s, until about 1883, Nathanael Herreshoff concentrated almost all of his attention on the development of light steam engines and on improving the construction of hulls, trying to reduce weight without sacrificing strength. Practically all of this innovative work was being done in connection with the light steam launches that the Herreshoff brothers were building. Although these early experiments were originally criticized by the yachting fraternity, many of today's small boats are still built with the techniques worked out at the Herreshoff boatyard more than 125 years ago. Proof of the Herreshoffs' expertise is that so many of their small boats are still in use, even though they were built lighter than those of their competitors.

Because small steam launches were hoisted up on the davits of ships, extreme lightness in both power plant and hull was paramount. The Herreshoff launches stood up better than the heavier ones made by other boatyards. The reason for their superior service was that heavier launches would suffer strains in being hoisted and lowered in a seaway. Light launches with steam-bent frames would cushion the shock of stresses that would damage an unyielding, rigidly constructed boat.

The Herreshoffs built many of these early launches for governmental agencies: the U.S. Navy, the U.S. Ordnance Department, the U.S. Coast Survey, and the U.S. Fish Commission. One of their early models, 22 feet long and 5 feet 3 inches abeam, was built between 1876 and 1878. It represented the first attempt at a modern powerboat. The greatest draft was a little aft of forefoot, and the greatest beam was near the stern, which was flat. The underwater shape was a gradual twist from bow to stern. This type of launch was said to have been very satisfactory, driving very easily into a moderate head sea. However, since Nathanael Herreshoff abandoned the model shortly after 1878, the sharp-bowed launches with wide flat sterns were probably proven to be unsuitable for all conditions.

The power plant used on the small launches built between 1876 and 1880 was a small coil boiler over a circular firebox and ash pit, the whole of which was enclosed by a cylindrical casing. The boiler, capable of making steam in only a few minutes, was a single-cylinder

A Herreshoff steam engine and boiler. Built in 1893 by Nathaniel G. Herreshoff for his personal use in a 22-foot launch, this steam engine is still in running condition. (Postcard.)

Herreshoff's British torpedo boat Hull No. 44. Inauspiciously referred to by her crew as "the Coffin," she was taken into the service as H.M. 2nd Class Torpedo Boat No. 63. (Courtesy Scientific American.*)*

engine of 3.5 inches bore and 7 inches stroke, producing about 5 horsepower. (It should be remembered that horsepower was developed from the energy of coal. While coal-generated horsepower is the same as the horsepower generated from gasoline or diesel, the volume of fuel required for that horsepower is different.) The whole operation at that time was neat, simple, light, reliable, and very economical.

One type of propeller used in the early Herreshoff launches and steamers was 24 inches in diameter and 36 inches in pitch. In the early 1870s, however, Nathanael Herreshoff designed a series of similar propellers that varied greatly in size but not much in shape. The small launches generally had two-bladed propellers, which were true screws—they had the same pitch throughout the blade, and each blade was slightly concave on the pressure side.

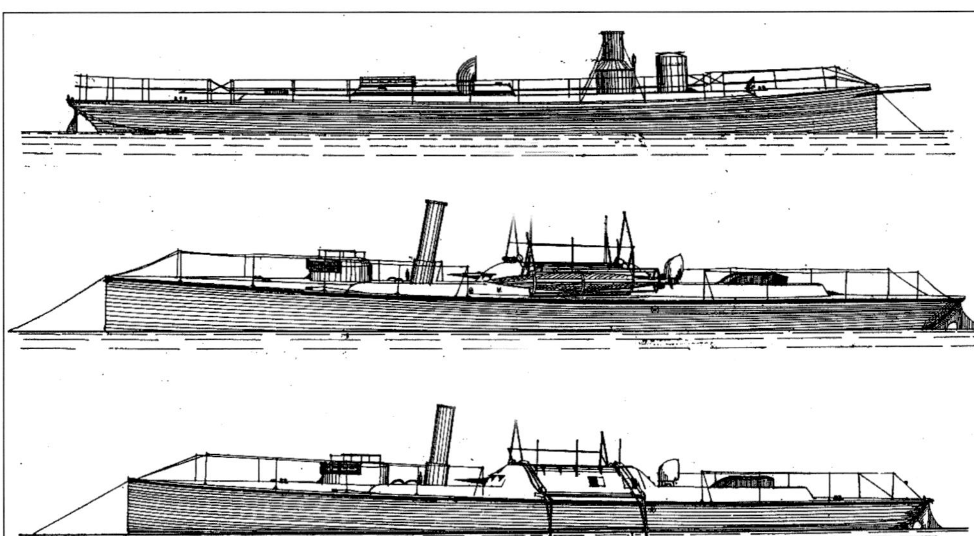

Thornycroft's torpedo boats.

When Nathanael Herreshoff was designing steam-driven craft, there were no commercial propellers made. Therefore, as long as the Herreshoff Manufacturing Company built steamers, it continued to make propellers of Nathanael Herreshoff's design.

During the Civil War, Americans on both sides of the conflict endeavored to develop superior fighting ships. One of the vessels favored as an offensive weapon was the stealthy spar torpedo boat. In 1864, Lt. William Cushing of the Union navy bravely faced a rain of Confederate shot to destroy the ironclad *Albemarle.* Cushing accomplished this with a fast steam launch armed only with an explosive charge mounted on the end of a long pike—a spar torpedo.

In the 1870s, experiments continued with high-speed torpedo boats, such as the Herreshoffs' *Lightning,* a double-ended spar torpedo boat. There were many other builders of small, steam-propelled boats in Europe and in England, with Thornycroft and Yarrow among the most successful. Thornycroft built some of the first fast launches, and Yarrow specialized in high-speed steamers and other light craft. However, these other early torpedo boats all had heavy fire tube boilers and rather heavy hulls, so they were not as fast as the torpedo boats and launches being designed at the same time by the Herreshoffs in Bristol, Rhode Island.

Some of the Herreshoff-built torpedo boats and others built by competing American yards took part in the war with Spain, but their use was mostly inconsequential to the effort. The boats were not assigned to missions to which they were best suited—that is, swift attack and picket duty. Most often they were dispatched to patrol and courier duty because their bunker capacity was too small to allow long periods at sea. They required frequent refueling and were too fragile for direct head-to-head combat with larger vessels.

The early torpedo boats did, however, provide valuable experience to future designers and builders. The development of the modern destroyer and torpedo technology can be laid directly to the first fledgling fleet of American torpedo boats.

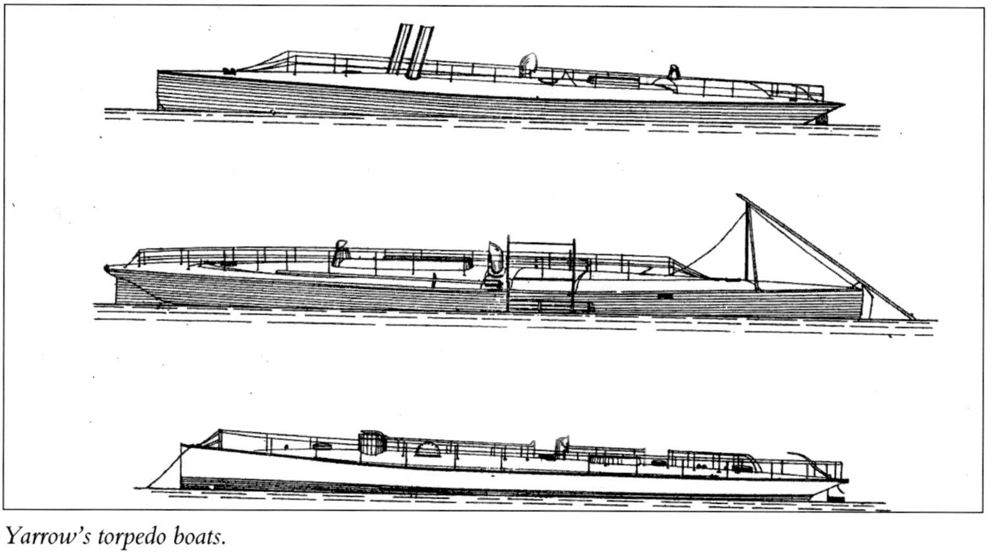

Yarrow's torpedo boats.

A spar torpedo in Newport Harbor. The spar torpedo boat was used with some success during the Civil War. As shown in the inset, the boat carried an explosive charge fastened to the end of a spar (pole), which was secured to the boat and rigged so that it could be projected forward or abeam and lowered well below the waterline of an enemy ship. (U.S. Navy photograph.)

The Herreshoff boatyard, c. *1890. (Period postcard.)*

Two
Prelude

During the Civil War, both sides in the conflict employed spar torpedoes in naval engagements, and both sides can be credited with developing innovative warships and strategies for employing them. After the war, however, technical development in the U.S. Navy waned and went through a period of stagnation. While foreign navies were building on the lessons learned from the American Civil War, Washington had become complacent.

The torpedo of that time was the spar torpedo. Carried at the end of a 20- to 25-foot-long spar, this type of torpedo was capable of being rigged at various angles. It could be brought in contact with the bottom of an enemy vessel by a steam launch or pulling boat and discharged by means of an electrical connection. For success, it was necessary to come alongside the enemy before discovery and disablement. In a time without searchlights or rapid-fire guns, this task was—on a dark or foggy night—less impossible than might be thought.

For some years, the torpedo remained as it was at the close of the war—the weapon of the regular pulling boats and steam launches of the man-of-war. Boats that served as the regular running boats in peacetime were provided with apparatus for using the spar torpedo in time of war. Early in the 1870s, it was proposed to construct small steam vessels for use as torpedo boats. These boats had a lightness of hull, fineness of lines, and exceptionally large source of motive power that would ensure a speed of 15 to 18 knots. A little before this, the Whitehead torpedo had been introduced and was being tested by all the European powers. It was this "automobile torpedo" that was destined to revolutionize ideas of torpedo warfare and make the construction of special torpedo vessels necessary.

With the invention of Whitehead's automobile torpedo, a suitable delivery platform for the weapon became a subject of navy study.[2] When coupled with the high-speed torpedo boat, the powerful torpedo (the first nonrecoil weapon capable of destroying an ironclad warship) was considered an inexpensive offensive weapon. In 1869, the first U.S. naval torpedo station was established on Goat Island in Newport Harbor for the experimentation, development, and manufacture of American- and foreign-designed torpedoes.[3]

Around the time special torpedo boats were beginning to be built, the Whitehead torpedo had made such progress as to find some advocates for its use. From the uncertainties attending the action of the early automobile torpedo and the demonstrated efficiency of the spar torpedo, the latter was often preferred to the former. Most of the early torpedo boats were originally provided with spar torpedoes and later fitted for the use of automobile torpedoes. The introduction of the rapid-fire gun was the death blow of the spar torpedo and emphasized the necessity for high-speed vessels designed especially to deliver the automobile torpedo. From this point on, the growth and improvement of the torpedo boat more than kept pace with its principal weapon.

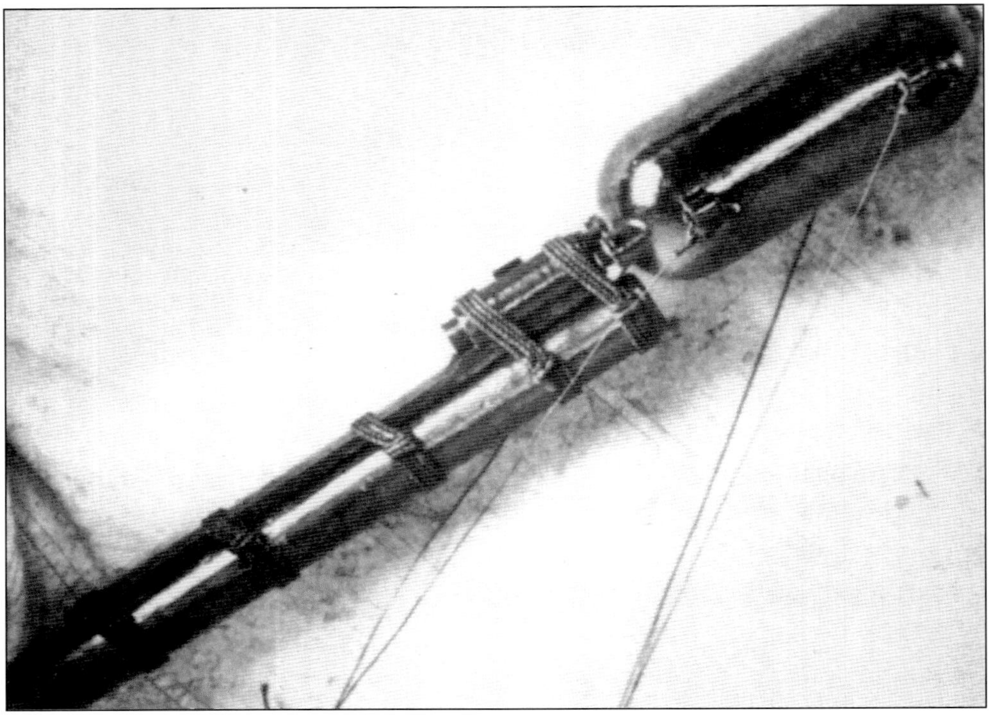

A period photograph of a spar torpedo with its triggering halyard. (NTS photograph.)

Adm. David Dixon Porter, a strong advocate for the building of naval craft to deliver the new self-propelled torpedo, almost single-handedly directed navy policy in the 1870s and 1880s. Admiral Porter was the guiding light for the building of the *Alarm* and the *Intrepid*—two experimental torpedo boats—and the 1876 Herreshoff spar torpedo boat *Lightning*.

For about 10 weeks during the summer of 1880, the U.S. Navy, under the direction of Commo. B.F. Isherwood, carried out extensive tests with two Herreshoff-built steam launches (Hull No. 62 and Hull No. 63) as well as a navy equivalent that had been built at the Washington Navy Yard. The U.S. Navy Board of Investigation—consisting of Commodore Isherwood, Commodore Zeller, and assistants from the U.S. Navy School of Marine Engineers—found the Herreshoff launches superior in every way when compared to the navy-designed launch.

The navy began to revive in 1881, when Admiral Porter managed to convene a naval advisory board. The board's job was to recommend programs of construction to the secretary of the navy. The board's goal (under Porter's insistence) was to modernize the U.S. Navy along the lines of European navies. Some of the world's traditional sea powers played dominant political roles with formidable fleets of torpedo boats and torpedo boat destroyers. From this time on, successive advisory boards and secretaries of the navy recommended to Congress ever-expanding programs for torpedo boat construction. In 1885, Secretary William C. Whitney said that 50 torpedo boats could be built for the price

A spar torpedo explosion in Newport Harbor, c. 1880. (Stereo view by J.A. Williams; courtesy Larry and Luana Rochette.)

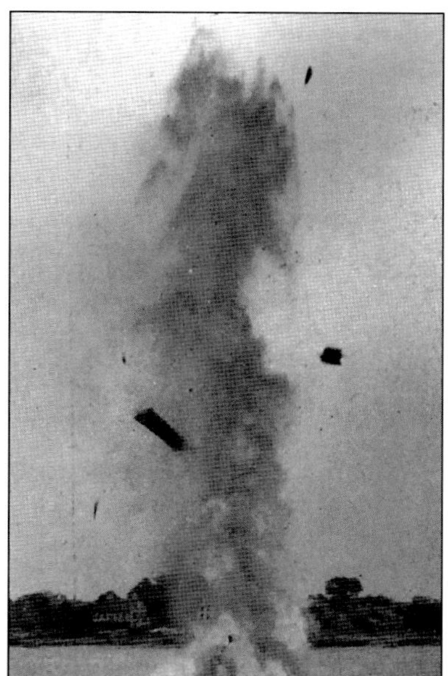

The explosive power of the spar torpedo can be clearly seen in this experimental detonation by the torpedo station in Newport Harbor.

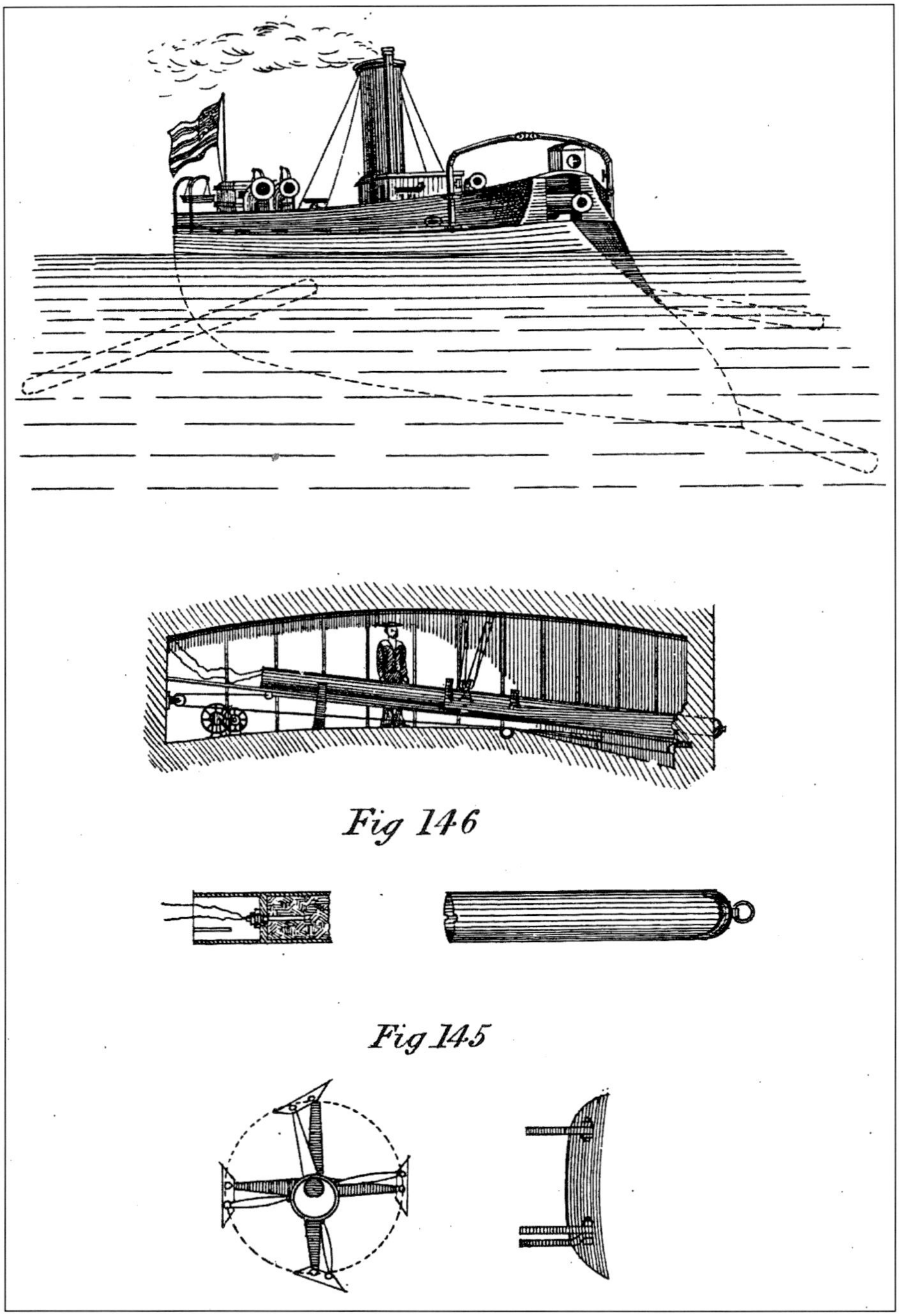

The Alarm. *The iron torpedo boat* Alarm *was designed by Adm. David Dixon Porter. The* Alarm *had a double bottom and watertight compartments; she carried one heavy gun on her bow and was provided with a ram and spar torpedoes. She had one spar extending directly in line with her keel, some 30 feet beyond the point of the ram. She maneuvered by use of the Mallory steering propeller, which functioned both as a rudder and a propeller.*

The torpedo boat Alarm. *The underwater shape of her ram can be seen in this period U.S. Navy photograph.*

of a single ironclad battleship. From the time of the construction of the torpedo launch *Lightning,* nothing was done toward providing torpedo boats for the navy until 1888. That year, the U.S. Navy Department purchased from the Herreshoff Manufacturing Company a fast wooden yacht, the *Stiletto,* and converted it for use as an experimental torpedo boat.

Nonetheless, it was not until August 1886 that Congress authorized funds to construct a seagoing torpedo boat. In little more than three years (in January 1890), the navy took possession of the Herreshoff-built Torpedo Boat No. 1, the *Cushing.* She was made of galvanized steel throughout and, at the time of her completion, was a good example of current practice.

Secretary Benjamin F. Tracy wanted 20 boats like the *Cushing,* but the navy's second boat was not authorized until mid-1890. That purchase was the *Ericsson,* a modified version of the *Cushing,* built to navy specifications by the Iowa Iron Works.

Still, Admiral Porter persisted. He wanted 20 torpedo boats of 150 feet, each with a speed of 26 knots. "These vessels," he said, "should be designed by Messrs. Herreshoff who, with their quadruple expansion engines, would have no difficulty in obtaining the necessary speed."

Further construction was not authorized until July 26, 1894, when the secretary of the navy was authorized enough funding "for the construction of one additional cruiser of the *Vesuvious* type" and as much as was necessary for the construction, armament, and equipment of three torpedo boats. Thus, the U.S. Navy's torpedo boat program finally became a reality. The 1894 construction program produced near replicas of the *Ericsson,*

The Cushing *(Torpedo Boat No. 1) in Newport Harbor. Old Fort Dumpling can be seen in the left background. (Courtesy* Scientific American.*)*

all built by the Columbian Iron Works to navy plans. Two of the second series (No. 6 and No. 7) were built in the Herreshoff shops to their own plans, and the third was built by the Moran Brothers in Seattle, Washington, to navy plans.

As the navy's engine designs gradually improved, boat speeds rose from 23 knots in the *Ericsson* to 24.5 in the Winslow (No. 5), and 26 in the *Rowan* (No. 8). The Herreshoffs guaranteed 27.5 knots in the *Porter* (No. 6) and in the *Dupont* (No. 7).[4]

In 1896, three seagoing boats (Nos. 9–11) were authorized in addition to six smaller and slower coastal harbor patrol boats (Nos. 12–17). Of the smaller boats (20 and 22.5 knots), the navy prepared the plans, although it was open to alternatives. In fact, the Herreshoff Manufacturing Company, the Columbian Iron Works, and Wolff & Zwicker were allowed to build their own designs. The Herreshoff effort resulted in the *Morris* (No. 14), the *Talbot* (No. 15), and the *Gwin* (No. 16), all delivered in early 1898.

During the last decade of the 19th century, the world's navies considered the torpedo boat primarily a coastal defense weapon. In the way of armament, torpedo boats relied on their torpedoes and on little in the way of guns. Generally, they were not very seaworthy because of their thin steel hulls and were thus best suited for restricted home water duty. In a report delivered by Assistant Navy Secretary Theodore Roosevelt on March 16, 1898, he said:

> We believe that a dozen small torpedo boats of the *Gwin* type should be ordered. These ought to be constructed in ninety days. Mr. Herreshoff says it would take about four months, but under pressure we think he could be made to guarantee that they would be done in ninety days.

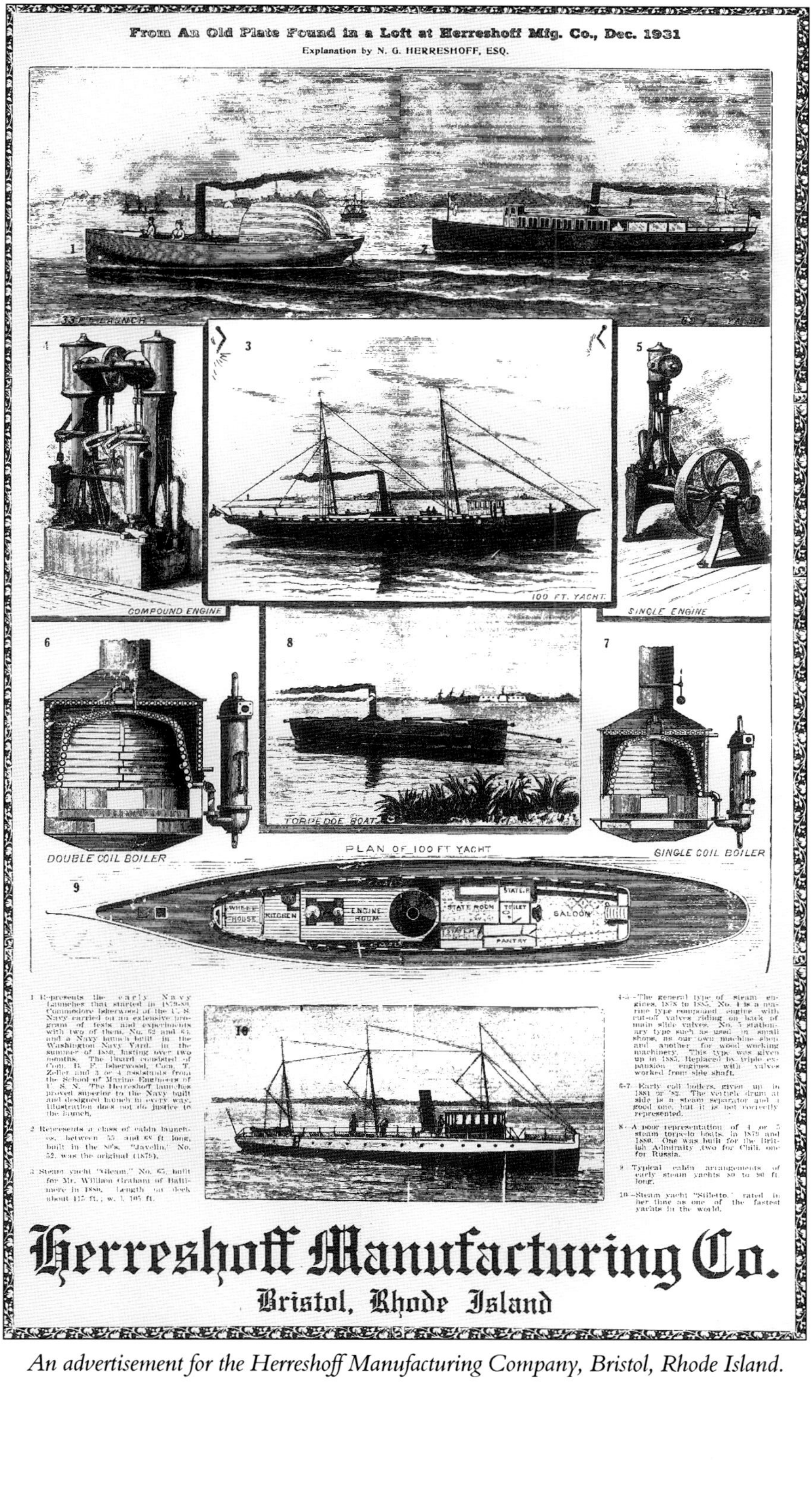

An advertisement for the Herreshoff Manufacturing Company, Bristol, Rhode Island.

In response to Roosevelt's recommendations, a new building program began. On May 4, 1898, Congress authorized the first of 16 torpedo boat destroyers and 12 torpedo boats of the seagoing type. Only four boats could be constructed by any one yard. The U.S. Navy Board of Construction recommended that the Herreshoff Manufacturing Company be awarded a contract for two of the torpedo boats. However, the U.S. Navy Department thought otherwise and, although no further navy vessels were ever again purchased directly from the Herreshoffs, their place in naval history was secured.

John Brown Herreshoff (left) and Nathanael Greene Herreshoff.

Three
Fast Launches and Spar Torpedo Boats

The Destruction of the *New Ironsides*

It is proper to make note of the first successful attack ever made by a steam torpedo boat upon an enemy vessel. The daring offensive action was that of the Confederate's small steam-driven iron boat the *David.* She was built to lie very low in the water so that when under way, her decks were awash, thus dramatically reducing her profile. Her armament was a spar torpedo.

On October 5, 1863, the Union frigate *New Ironsides* became the first vessel to be destroyed by a specially constructed torpedo launching platform. During the fight, the accurate and punishing fire from the *New Ironsides* drove Confederate gunners to take cover, allowing the Union army to do its work unmolested. The Union ship's dominance of Charleston's waters made her a prime target for the Confederate navy's torpedo boat. Shortly after nine that evening, the *David,* operated by a crew of four, boldly steamed into Charleston Harbor and headed directly to her target. The lookouts aboard the *New Ironsides* spied a low-lying boat approaching. The only answer to the hail of "Boat, ahoy!" was a musket shot followed almost instantly by an explosion close alongside. The powerful blast, which shook the vessel to her core, threw a great quantity of water into the air. This was followed by a hail of bullets directed at the adventurous little craft as she drifted into the darkness. A boat was sent from the severely wounded frigate in search of the aggressor. Two of the *David*'s crew were found, but there was no sight of the boat itself.

After the war, it was learned that the *David* had not sunk but was abandoned. Her pilot, who could not swim, clung to the boat. The engineer, who floated nearby, saw that the boat was not sinking and swam to her. The two crew members kindled her fires and steamed back to Charleston.

The *New Ironsides* was out of action for the duration of the siege of Charleston.

Lt. William Barker Cushing and the *Albemarle*

The Confederates were building one or more ironclads in nearly every blockaded port. One of these, the *Albemarle,* was victorious in several battles with Union navy vessels in the sounds of North Carolina. Navy strategists declared that her continued existence greatly endangered Union supremacy in Charleston's waters.

The night of October 27, 1863, was stormy when Lt. William Cushing and his 14 volunteers set out on their 8-mile trip up the Roanoke in their 30-foot steam launch. The

The destruction of the New Ironsides *by the Confederate steam launch spar torpedo boat* David, *off Charleston, 1864. (From* Scribner's St. Nicholas Magazine, *1893.)*

Lt. William Barker Cushing.

Albemarle was known to lie somewhere at Plymouth Landing. Both banks of the 150-yard-wide river were in the hands of the Confederates.

Cushing's torpedo boat towed a ship's cutter (whale boat) manned by two officers and 11 men, the supporting force for Cushing's daring scheme. He planned nothing less than to cut the *Albemarle* from her mooring and bring her triumphantly down the river to Adm. David D. Porter, his commander.

Under cover of a driving rain, Cushing and his intrepid crew proceeded phantomlike up the river. At 2:30 in the morning, they came abreast of the *Southfield,* a Union gunboat taken earlier in the year by the *Albemarle.* Now her wreck was used as a Confederate picket station. Cushing's launch stole past, not 20 yards away, undiscovered.

The object of Cushing's plan was lying only another mile up river.

Soon, Cushing and his raiders could make out the shape of the ironclad. As the little steamer approached, its bow bumped against something, causing a loud crunching sound. Cushing ascertained the obstacle in his path was a boom of floating logs surrounding the

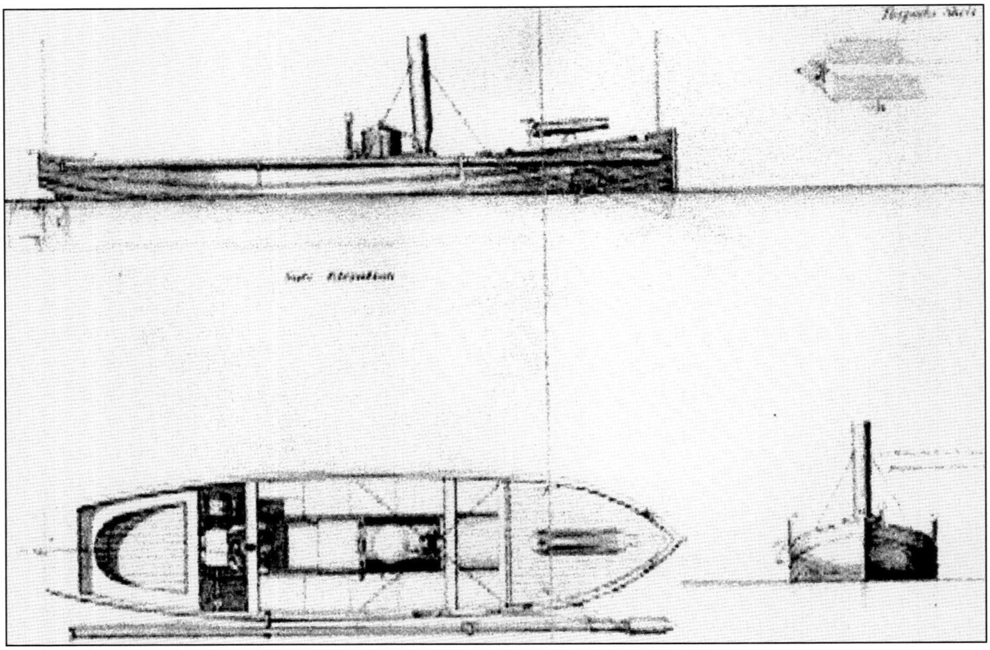

This illustration is representative of the type of steam launch used as a torpedo boat by Lt. William Barker Cushing to destroy the Albemarle.

Albemarle to protect her against the possibility of just such an attack. The noise the steamer made roused the sleeping Confederates. Suddenly, the fires on both sides of the river flared up and a voice shouted, "Boat ahoy!"

His surprise attack having been discovered, Cushing commanded the cutter to cast off to drift downriver toward the wreck of the *Southfield.* The shore and the ironclad were alive with shouting Confederates as their muskets blazed, sending bullets in the direction of the little steamer.

"Full steam, now!" barked Cushing and made another run for the *Albemarle.* This time the launch straddled the boom. Her bow rose high into the air and her propeller thrashed wildly for a moment. Then she was over and alongside the ironclad.

Cushing, far forward, planted his cumbersome torpedo on the end of a 16-foot spar, below the *Albemarle*'s waterline, where the overhanging steel-plate armor did not reach. Then, one of the *Albemarle*'s gunports flew open, and the 15 men in the launch were looking straight into the muzzle of a 100-pound rifle gun. "Surrender or die!" came the command.

Two of Cushing's men dove into the river at the shout. The gun belched. A sailor standing beside Cushing cried out and fell forward, mortally wounded. The rest of the crew ducked and heard the full charge of canister and a small shot whistle past their ears.

Almost immediately after the cannon blast, a second dull roar came. Cushing had pulled the trigger lanyard of his torpedo. The concussion threw the steam launch into the air, and more of the crew tumbled into the water. The *Albemarle,* with a gaping wound in her side, slowly began to keel over and threatened to roll right on top of the launch.

This dramatic illustration shows the ironclad monitor Tecumseh *after being struck by a torpedo during Admiral Farragut's 1864 attack upon the forts at Mobile. (From* Scribner's St. Nicholas Magazine, *1893.)*

"Swim for it, boys!" shouted Cushing to the crew members not already in the river.

Cushing followed his men; he dove in and did not surface until he had passed under the boom. Swimming downriver, he repeatedly submerged as the whole surface of the river around him was plowed up by grapeshot and musket bullets. He came ashore on a swampy peninsula 2 miles from the wreckage of his historic adventure.

Herreshoff Fast Steam Launches

The speed and performance of the Herreshoff-designed steam launches came to the attention of several governments, and it was not long before the Herreshoffs began building spar torpedo boats. These boats were about 56 feet long and only 6 feet 6 inches abeam. They were almost perfect double-enders—that is, they ran either end first and at nearly the same speed. Previous to the Herreshoff double-enders, spar torpedo boats carried only one spar with its bomb attached in place over the bow, but the Herreshoff double-enders carried two spar torpedoes, one in place at each end.

These little torpedo boats ran very smoothly and quietly up to a speed of about 21 knots. One of the most remarkable attributes of the boats was an ability to slow down or stop completely and quickly. This could be done because the boats were very light, had relatively large propellers, and the engines could be instantly reversed (even with the throttle wide open).

The propellers, placed near the middle of the boats, did not cavitate. These craft could stop within a few lengths (even when running at full speed) and within seconds could be

Ericsson's Destroyer *as shown on a period advertising card. John Ericsson was born on July 31, 1803, in Vermland, Sweden. He is best known for devising and building the Civil War ironclad* Monitor. *A prolific inventor, Ericsson advanced maritime science in many ways, perfecting the screw propeller and other devices that played a significant part in advancing naval engineering. Ericsson died in New York City on March 8, 1890.*

going 20 knots in the opposite direction—a most valuable accomplishment in the life-and-death heroics of launching a spar torpedo.

Another unusual feature of these torpedo-delivery craft was that the propeller shaft ran on a slight curve so that the engine, which was forward of the boiler, was mounted on an angle, while the shaft at the propeller was more horizontal. The shaft, which was made of ether steel or iron, ran its full length in a snug-fitting, well-lubricated brass tube. One could say the shaft ran in a continuous bearing, so there was almost no friction. The long strut that supported the curved propeller shaft was made of brass or bronze plates that acted as a streamlined keel condenser.

The boats were small and light enough to be hoisted aboard a man-of-war. They were very reliable when maintained and served as good sea boats at a reduced speed.

THE *LIGHTNING* AND THE *SPRAY*

As the U.S. Navy Department took notice of the Herreshoff designs, the fast steam launch was considered by naval authorities to be the vehicle of choice for delivering the new torpedo weapons.

In November 1875, the U.S. Navy Bureau of Ordnance ordered the torpedo boat *Lightning* (Hull No. 20) to be built for the cost of $5,000: "The speed [is] to be 19 m.p.h., for one hour, using salt water, and [you are ordered] to commence the work without delay." This was the first torpedo boat purchased by the U.S. Navy, although it had previously converted steam launches to torpedo boats. Herreshoff's *Lightning* was a long, narrow, double-ended launch, partly decked. She was 58 feet long, 6 feet 3 inches abeam, and 3 feet 2 inches

The Confederacy's coal-burning, semisubmersible spar torpedo boat David, *pictured here, was privately built and donated to the Confederate navy by Theodore Stoney of Charleston, South Carolina. During the Civil War, both the Union and Confederate navies developed and employed new technology to build radical new weapons of war. The Confederates built a number of small steam-powered launches, generally referred to as "Davids" to attack Union warships. The Davids, operating with their decks awash to reduce their profiles, had spar torpedoes mounted on an underwater spar affixed to the bow. These small launches conducted sneak attacks, generally at night, against anchored Union ships on blockade duty.*

The Herreshoff-built spar torpedo boat Lightning *at the Newport torpedo station. The Civil War established the torpedo as the weapon of choice, but much time and talent was devoted to its improvement after the war. A torpedo attack still mainly relied on "a bag of powder on the end of a pole," as it has been called. The greatest gains were made in the speed of the launches and in the method of firing the torpedo. The* Lightning *made a speed of 24 knots. The great peculiarity of these Herreshoff boats was their boiler, in which steam could be raised to working pressure in five minutes or less and could be kept at that pressure without difficulty. The propeller and rudder of the Herreshoff boats had a peculiar arrangement, and the whole boat, built of wood, was so light that it could be stopped in its own length when going at full speed. Herreshoff boats steered just as well when going astern as when going ahead. (U.S. Navy photograph.)*

Capt. K.R. Breese, inspector of ordnance, U.S. Navy. Breese served as commanding officer of the Naval Torpedo Station at Newport from 1875 to 1878.

draft. She carried conventional spar torpedoes. Her top speed was an impressive 22 knots, a record that had never been equaled by any boat of her length at that time.

The *Lightning*'s last official trial run took place on Wednesday, May 26, 1876, under the supervision of Lt. George A. Converse. Converse, a navy instructor assigned to the Naval Torpedo Station at Newport, acted as the government's inspector. The *Lightning* made the run from Usher's buoy in Bristol to Bishop's Rock buoy in Newport—a distance of 10.25 miles—in the record time of 26 minutes and 45 seconds. The time on her return run was greater because it was hampered by the blowing off of the after-steam gauge while above Bishop's Rock. Without stopping, the boat was repaired and steam was kept up to 80 pounds.

Worn out and no longer in service, the *Lightning* was hauled up sometime before 1889 at the Newport torpedo station. As history shows, America was already outclassed in torpedo boat technology, for European navies were outbuilding the U.S. Navy at an average of about 165 to 1. By 1877, England had built the high-speed torpedo boat ram *Lightning,* and others were planned or in construction. By 1892, England had 186 fast torpedo boats, France, 220; Russia, 152; Germany, 143; and Italy, 129.

In 1879, Capt. K.R. Breese, inspector of ordnance and commanding officer of the Newport torpedo station from 1875 to 1878, inspected a new steam launch just constructed by the Herreshoff Manufacturing Company at nearby Bristol. Evidently his report to the U.S. Navy Department was favorable because, on May 16, 1879, the Bureau of Ordnance directed the purchase of this 42-foot launch, the *Spray.* The *Spray* was used for spar torpedo experiments for a short time but was eventually pressed into service as a ferry between the navy's installations on the islands in Narragansett Bay.

THE *VISION* AND THE *ESTELLE*

Buoyed by the success of its spar torpedo boat *Lightning,* the Herreshoff Manufacturing Company built a trial horse with a new type of coil engine. The *Vision,* as she was called, was extremely fast and brought international attention to the Bristol firm. For an early trial run in November 1877, a group of federal agents was invited to participate. After the guests had stepped aboard the narrow craft, with James Herreshoff (brother of John and Nathanael Herreshoff) at the controls, the boat was gunned to life. She quickly leapt to 15 knots, pushing the guests into their seats. The agents left the demonstration sore of behind but considerably impressed.

The *Vision* could move as fast as the *Lightning* and could be armed to work as either a torpedo boat or a gunboat. The U.S. Navy, as it turned out, was "not interested," although the navies of some foreign governments were.

The impression made that day was not lost on New York lawyer Herman Kobbe, who was also an unregistered agent for the insurgent government of Cuba. He immediately placed an order for a 120-foot steamer that could match the speed of the *Vision.* Kobbe put down cash to begin the work and promised a bonus for quick delivery of the boat, which was to be a cargo carrier called the *Estelle.*

At 120 feet in length and 16 feet abeam, the *Estelle* was too big to be built at the Bristol boatyard, so the hull construction was contracted to Job Terry's boatyard in Fall River, Massachusetts, some 10 miles east of Bristol. When the hull was completed, John Brown used one of his 40-foot steamers to tow the *Estelle* to Bristol, where the engine, boiler, and other marine equipment were installed.

It was known that the *Estelle* was destined for use in the Caribbean, and it was later learned that Herman Kobbe had contracted for the fast boat on behalf of a group of Cuban gunrunning rebels. Since Washington had an eye on Cuba, it was also watching the progress of the *Estelle*'s construction. In December 1877, U.S. Revenue Cutter *Dexter* arrived at Bristol, anchored in the harbor, and kept watch on the Herreshoff dock and on

The Herreshoff-built steamer Estelle *anchored at the State Street pier in Bristol Harbor.*

The U.S. Revenue Service cutter Dexter *(left) and the Herreshoff steamer* Estelle *in Bristol Harbor, 1877.*

the *Estelle,* which would soon begin its test runs. The *Dexter*'s orders were simple: "Do not let the boat leave the dock."

Shortly before Christmas 1877, the *Estelle,* with armed government agents from the *Dexter* aboard, made her trial run from Bristol to Brenton's Reef Light Ship at the Newport Harbor entrance. She ran about 60 miles beyond Brenton Point into the Atlantic before returning. The total elapsed time of the run was about six hours.

The owners were represented by Kobbe and a "rough looking Spaniard" who was to operate the boat upon acceptance. The *Estelle,* which made a better speed than her contracted 16 knots, was accepted by the owner's representatives and paid for. She was immediately seized by U.S. Treasury Department agents and then secured at Bristol Wharf. Part of her engine was taken as insurance that she would not leave.

The *Estelle* spent considerable time in government custody. In June 1878, she was released to the lawyer Kobbe, who sold her to a man from Washington, D.C. The *Estelle*'s new owner employed her as a mail carrier and ultimately as a towboat at the mouth of the Mississippi River, where she was known as the fastest tug in the area. (As a curious footnote to this story, one cannot help but wonder why the Cuban's agent Kobbe was allowed to take possession of, and eventually sell, the boat.)

The *XPDNC*

The original model for the *XPDNC* (shorthand for *expediency*), made *c.* 1878, was intended to be used as a steam torpedo boat hull, although it was never built as such. The *XPDNC* was eventually built for Frank H. Crocker in 1904 as a gasoline launch racer. On September 14 and 16, 1905, she won the National Trophy in a series of races on the Hudson River in New York State. The races consisted of three 30-knot heats in which she made an average speed of about 28 knots.

Marine architect L. Francis Herreshoff, son of Nathanael Herreshoff, thought very highly of the *XPDNC* model. "But what is even more remarkable," he wrote in his book

Captain Nat Herreshoff, "is the fact that some of the latest torpedo boat destroyers—those now in use [*c.* 1950]—are very similar in underwater shape, and when the destroyer finally gets to this exact model, it will be nearing perfection."

Foreign Government Craft

Between 1878 and 1880, the Herreshoffs attempted to break into the booming torpedo boat market. They produced five double-ended, whale-backed, highly maneuverable craft to be armed with spar torpedoes. These boats were based on the *Lightning* model. For several years until about 1885, the Herreshoffs built high-speed launches for both the French and English governments—109 for the French and 73 for the English. These craft have become known historically as the Vedette Class, measuring 40 to 50 feet in length. In the building of fast craft for foreign navies, the Herreshoffs had no peer.

Of the four Vedette boats built for the U.S. Navy, two were to be carried by the *Maine* and two by the *Texas.* The Vedette boats were originally intended to be carried on the decks of battleships. However, carrying such cumbrous things on the decks of ships proved to be problematic, and the plan was largely abandoned in nearly all navies.

Hull No. 44.

The first of these Herreshoff-built spar torpedo boats, designated Hull No. 44, was a demonstration prototype completed in July 1878. She was 59 feet 6 inches long and 7 feet 6 inches abeam. Excluding the midship centerboard and screw, she had a draft of 2 feet 9 inches and was the first boat of her kind to use as much steel or iron in the hull. Below the sheer line, she had wood planking over steel frames, but the upper sides and deck were made of 1/16-inch steel. The boat had a compound engine with a stroke of 10 inches and bores of 6 and 10.5 inches. The coil boiler was 4 feet in diameter and had 3-inch-diameter

The Herreshoff steam launch Ibis, Jr. *This vessel was built for British customer George R. Dunnell in 1878–1879. (Courtesy* Scientific American.*)*

tubes about 30 feet long, using a working pressure of 160 pounds. The weight of the craft was only 6 tons, but the weight approached 7.5 tons with a crew of four, fuel, and torpedoes. She ran the same speed astern as ahead and turned in a circle about three times her length. Her expected speed of 16 knots was easily met. Her deck was fully enclosed and clear, except for a smokestack and a small turret aft for the helmsman.

The Herreshoff brothers took this torpedo boat to England along with a 29-foot, double-ended launch, the *Ibis, Jr.,* for delivery to London customer George R. Dunnell, a wealthy entrepreneur. Dunnell bought Hull No. 44 on speculation for the British navy.

The Herreshoffs' American crew ran trials of the torpedo boat on the Thames River before a gathering of senior naval officers and the first lord of the admiralty. Subsequently, at the instigation of Chief Naval Constructor Nathaniel Barnaby, the Royal Navy purchased the boat from Dunnell for thorough evaluation.

Known to her British crew as "the Coffin," she was taken into the service as H.M. 2nd Class Torpedo Boat No. 63. In 1881, she was used for training at the Vernon Torpedo School. She returned in 1884 to the Portsmouth Steam Reserve still under trial and not yet fitted with torpedo gear. Apparently there was some doubt of her stability. In 1887, she reportedly collided with a tug and suffered damage to her bow. In 1888, she was expended as a target at Portsmouth to test the effect of shell fire on a torpedo boat. Under close-range fire for the best part of a day, she took 26 hours to sink.

Hull Nos. 53, 55, and 60.

Herreshoff Hull No. 53 was completed in June 1879 for the government of Peru. Hull No. 55 was completed in August that year and Hull No. 60 in December. These double-enders were similar to Hull No. 44, but without the sheet steel superstructure. The boat was 59 feet long and 7 feet abeam, with a 5-foot draft. The machinery was aft, and the 33.5-inch-diameter driving screw was forward of amidships. These craft were built in prefabricated sections for final construction on the West Coast. Hull No. 60 was never delivered to Peru. She was left in the Herreshoffs' hands at the end of the 1879–1881 Peruvian-Chilean War and never found a buyer. Hull No. 60 was stored in the open on the Herreshoff family farm, Point Pleasant at Poppasquash, where she remained a local curiosity, slowly deteriorating. She lasted until *c.* 1910.

Hull No. 64.

One of the last spar torpedo boats built by the Herreshoff Manufacturing Company was Hull No. 64, constructed in 1880 for the Russian navy. Some 59 feet long and 6 feet 6 inches abeam, the boat had a 4-foot 7-inch draft. She made a record speed for those days of 23 knots on her trial run. Her double cedarwood hull was higher at the ends than the Herreshoffs' previous spar torpedo boats. This was achieved by having depressions or launching ways on her four quarters so that she could carry four spar torpedoes. Although this craft had several hatches, she was run and steered mostly from below deck with only the helmsman's head above deck. She was more streamlined than any other craft of her kind at the time.

The last of the double-enders, this craft is not listed in Moissev's list of Russian warships of 1861–1948. This suggests that she was never commissioned as an operational ship after running trials.

Half models of Herreshoff products. Shown are the Sport *(top),* Leila *(center), and the Russian navy's Herreshoff-built Hull No. 64. (Courtesy Hart Nautical Collection, MIT Museum.)*

In the winter of 1915, while Nathanael Herreshoff was in Bermuda, his brother John negotiated with the Russian government for a number of high-speed seagoing torpedo boats. The deal with Russia was the largest that John ever signed and the largest ever to be consigned to the Herreshoff boatyard. John knew this contract would garner work from other foreign governments that were arming against the imperial German submarine threat.

When Nathanael heard about the deal from his brother, he was not impressed. "The transaction is practically complete," John told Nathanael. "It only needs your signature." Russian money had been deposited and construction was ready to begin, but Nathanael put a stop to it. He reminded John of their mutual dislike for doing business with government and of their original agreement that the cost of doing business would never exceed the amount of money on hand.

The *Stiletto*

The Herreshoff brothers had grown prosperous by 1885 and decided to build a high-speed steam yacht. The boat—named *Stiletto* for her long, slender, tapered shape—was launched into Bristol Harbor on February 25, 1885. The boat was 94 feet in length, with an 11-foot 6-inch beam and a 5-foot draft. She was of wooden construction.

In building this boat, the Herreshoffs combined lightness with strength. The framing was done with white oak, and the keel was made of two lengths that were scarfed and bolted together. The garboards were side-bolted to the keel. The frames—spaced 15 inches, extending from the gunwale to the keel—were securely bolted to the keel and the garboards. Plank floors extended across the keel and to the frames they were bolted to. The frames were strung together by a thick strake 2 feet above the waterline, a top strake, and

The Stiletto *test firing a Howell torpedo in the Sakonnet River, Tiverton, Rhode Island. Operating as an experimental torpedo firing platform, the* Stiletto *had a torpedo tube mounted in her bow in 1892, and evaluations of the Mark 1 Howell torpedo were conducted in the Sakonnet River, Tiverton, Rhode Island. The new "automobile torpedo" could only run in a straight line. By necessity, therefore, the boat had to aim herself at the target before firing her missile. (U.S. Navy photograph.)*

a gutter strake lapping over the top strake and the ends of the deck beams. The stem and stern post were of white oak siding. The hull was strapped diagonally with iron straps to prevent working and twisting. The straps in the wake of the engine room and fire room were of extra strength and crossed in opposite directions outside the frames and inside the planking. The oak deck beams were fastened to the frames by malleable iron knees, lightened by holes and bolted through. The side planking was of two thicknesses. The inner planks consisted of white pine, the outer of yellow pine. The deck planking was in two thicknesses of white pine. The seams were not caulked, but a layer of white lead was placed between the two courses.

The boat was constructed with five bulkheads divided into six watertight compartments. The collision bulkhead was placed 7.5 feet behind the forward perpendicular, with the anchor chain being stowed in the compartment formed by this bulkhead. The second compartment, 24 feet long, served as the captain's cabin as well as a place to house the steering gear. The third, 18.5 feet in length, was the boiler room. The engine room, 11 feet long, occupied the fourth compartment. In the fifth, 24 feet from bulkhead to bulkhead, were the galley and crew's quarters. A storeroom, 5 feet long, occupied the sixth compartment.

One entered the second compartment through the conning tower. The third, fourth, and fifth were accessible by hatchways, and the sixth through a manhole. The fire room hatch cover was fitted with a spring catch that could be opened from above or below, and egress was easy in case of accident.

The interior of the boat received its light during the day through the hatches and 15 deadlights on each side, and at night by oil lamps.

The conning tower, about 4 feet in diameter, stood almost 3 feet above the level of the deck and had glazed windows all around for a 360-degree view. From a platform in the conning tower, the helmsman had conveniently at hand the steering handles, apparatus for signaling the engine room, and the whistle lever.

A clever design allowed the craft to be steered by hand or by steam at the discretion of the helmsman. In the fire room on the starboard side was a steam steering cylinder with a stroke of 24 inches. The steering wheel was attached to a horizontal spindle, the forward end of which had a small geared wheel. The spindle could be pushed slightly forward or pulled aft in its bearings and locked in either position by a small drop pawl. When pushed forward, the geared wheel engaged with the teeth of the rack. When aft, it engaged with multiplying gears connected with the rack. The latter position, giving more power to the wheel, was used in steering by hand only. Whenever the wheel was turned to starboard or to port, the spindle worked to one side or the other, and the valve was moved to open the forward or after-steam ports of the cylinder. When rotation of the wheel ceased, the spindle resumed its middle position and the valve was centered. Thus, the steam steering gear was always attached, and it was only necessary to turn on steam to the cylinder when its use was desired.

The Stiletto *alongside the Elm Street Pier, Newport Rhode Island, 1889, after a collision with a steam launch. (U.S. Navy photograph.)*

The Hudson River steamer Mary Powell. *The so-called Queen of the Hudson, shown here in a period picture postcard, relinquished her title after losing a celebrated 1885 race with the Herreshoff yacht* Stiletto.

The *Stiletto* had an unusual engine designed especially for the boat. It was a compound engine with a stroke of 12 inches and bores of 12 and 21 inches. It generated 359 horsepower. The boat's boiler was a step between the coil boiler and the three-drum water tube boiler, which was later adopted. The *Stiletto,* which could reportedly maintain a speed of 20 knots, once made a run of 8 hours at 26.5 knots at a time when such speeds were not yet available in boats sold to the general public.

Five tons of coal would drive the *Stiletto* 112 miles at a speed of 18 knots per hour. The same amount would drive her 515 miles at a speed of 11 knots. Each additional ton of coal increased the three-fourths-inch mean draft and added about 20 miles to the range at the former speed and about 100 miles at the latter.

After being run as a private yacht, the *Stiletto* was shown off on June 10, 1885, in a famous race against the Hudson River side-wheeler *Mary Powell,* dubbed "the Queen of the Hudson." In this race, the *Stiletto* beat the *Mary Powell* by six minutes in a run from the foot of West Twenty-third Street to Tarrytown. The following day, the *Stiletto* raced in the American Yacht Club Regatta. The *Stiletto* made the run from Larchmont to New London in 4 hours, 13 minutes, and 31 seconds, beating her chief rival, the *Atalanta,* by 40 minutes and 19 seconds. She was not awarded the prize, however, as the judges decided that she had not rounded the buoy at the finish. While this was a fatal tactical error, it was inconsequential in the face of the boat's impressive performance.

The *Frank Leslie Illustrated Newspaper* said of the June 11 race:

The Stiletto *in her celebrated race against the* Atalanta.

> When the racing yachts got outside the Narrows, there, with the unexpectedness of the *Flying Dutchman,* appeared the little black-and-white steam-yacht, with the dagger in her flag. She cut through the water, throwing two delicate lines of silvery spray off her sides, fifteen feet from her knife-edged bow, and was lost to sight in a few minutes.[5]

Although a diminutive craft—only 95 feet long with a waterline length of just 90 feet and a beam of 11 feet—the *Stiletto* made the highest recorded speed for a boat of her length and displacement over a measured nautical mile course. She also made the highest recorded speed for a three-hour trial for a boat of her displacement carrying a load in coal, water, crew, anchors and gear, and dead weight accounting for a third of that displacement.

The *Stiletto* was purchased by the U.S. Navy under an act of Congress dated March 3, 1887. She entered service in July 1888 and was assigned to the Naval Torpedo Station at Newport, on Goat Island.

The Herreshoff brothers designed and built several other trial horses for their innovative engines. One of them, a new speedy steam-yacht, the *Now Then,* was built for Norman L. Munro. The following letter from John Herreshoff to Comdr. C.F. Goodrich at the Newport torpedo station, was prompted by a report of the boat's progress in a short news item in the *New York Herald* on the same date as the letter.

Bristol, R. I.
July 13th, 1887
Comdr. Goodrich, U.S.N.
Torpedo Station
Newport, R.I.

Dear Sir,
After you left here Monday the "Now Then" made a very satisfactory run over the measured mile with pressure at 220lbs even. All of the [illegible] were within a range of a few seconds: the mean of the 3 pairs being at the rate of 23.005 statute miles per hour.

Yesterday, I went with the owner, and family to New York making the run from Fort Adams to foot of east 24th St. in 7 hours 4 minutes: for the first 2 hours 190lbs pressure, the balance 210lbs consumption being 4900lbs: machinery and boiler worked perfectly, and without apparent effort. The tide being fair about 2/3 of the way, which was nearly offset by high winds in the sound.

The item printed in the New York Herald of today is correct.

We expect to have the Stiletto ready for inspection on Saturday. We have heard nothing from the Secretary regarding her.

Respectfully,
John B. Herreshoff

The following document, addressed to Comdr. C.F. Goodrich at the Newport torpedo station, is logged as document 592. It was received on May 28, 1888, as "Authorizing the acceptance of the *Stiletto.*"

Navy Department
Washington, May 25, 1888

Sir:
You are hereby authorized and directed to accept delivery from The Herreshoff Manufacturing Company, of Bristol, R.I., of the vessel known as the "Stiletto" intended for use as a Torpedo Boat, and which has been purchased by authority of an act of Congress. After receiving the vessel you will, until further instructed, take

proper care and custody of the same.

A public bill, in triplicate, for the amount of the purchase money, viz.: $25,000, has been forwarded to Mr. John B. Herreshoff, treasurer of said Company, with the request that, after the triplicates shall have been duly recited, he will cause the same to be handed to you. He has also been informed that you are authorized to receive the vessel and that paymeny [*sic*] of said bill will be made by the Pay Officer at the Station.

Very respectfully,
W.A. Whitney
Secretary of the Navy.

Initial plans were to use this craft for testing spar torpedoes; but, with the development of the Howell automobile torpedo, the *Stiletto* was converted to become the navy's first torpedo boat capable of launching self-propelled torpedoes. At one point, plans were contemplated to fit the boat with two bow torpedo tubes, directly in line with the keel, but this plan was abandoned in favor of the better one of having a torpedo gun mounted forward, on deck, and capable of train so that torpedoes could be discharged in any direction within an arc of 180 degrees.

Designated as Wooden Torpedo Boat No. 1, the *Stiletto* displaced about 31,000 pounds. Her official navy speed was 18.2 knots. Purchased for experimental evaluation, the *Stiletto*

A Mark 1 Howell torpedo on the deck of the Stiletto, *Naval Torpedo Station at Newport, 1898. The* Stiletto*'s narrow beam is clearly visible. (U.S. Navy photograph.)*

The Stiletto *steaming in Narragansett Bay with her full complement on deck, 1898.*

The Stiletto *"on parade" in New York with the Atlantic Fleet. (From* The American Navy: Cuba and Hawaii, *1898.)*

The Stiletto *patrolling her station in Rhode Island Sound.*

was based in Newport throughout her career. A torpedo tube was installed in her bow in 1892, and experiments were conducted using the Mark I Howell automobile torpedo. During this period, the Hotchkiss Ordnance Company of Bridgeport and Providence operated for about five years (until 1898) a torpedo test barge on a firing range in the Sakonnet River.

In May 1893, Lt. F.H. Paine, a representative from the Naval Torpedo Station at Newport, contracted men in Tiverton, Rhode Island, to build and maintain a large raft in the river. The raft, from which torpedo experiments were conducted, was nestled in the northeast corner of Tiverton Basin at Mackerel Cove, under the projection of the railroad bridge to Aquidneck Island and Newport.

The *Queen City,* a steam ferryboat that plied Narragansett Bay between Providence and Sakonnet Point, became a torpedo transport delivering weapons to be tested to a place called Humphrey's Wharf.

A few of the local boys found employment at the station, and it became one of the showplaces on the river, reported Charles J. Sumner in a 1940s article in the *Providence Journal Bulletin.* "The Herreshoff wooden-hulled torpedo boat *Stilletto* [*sic*] was a frequent visitor," wrote Sumner, with many shots made from her deck, some broadside to the range. He continued, "How she was able to make the turn in the narrow fairway I never could understand. It always looked as if she would roll over in making the turn at high speed, but of course she never did."

During 1897, the boat was modified to burn fuel oil, but results of subsequent trials were disappointing, and the experiment was not repeated. The *Stiletto,* struck from the navy's list of vessels on January 27, 1911, was sold in Newport on July 18, 1911, to James F. Nolan of East Boston for scrapping. She is still considered by many marine engineers to have been the first high-speed steam yacht of her type.

SCIENTIFIC AMERICAN

[Entered at the Post Office of New York, N. Y., as Second Class Matter. Copyrighted, 1889, by Munn & Co.]

A WEEKLY JOURNAL OF PRACTICAL INFORMATION, ART, SCIENCE, MECHANICS, CHEMISTRY, AND MANUFACTURES.

Vol. LX.—No. 18. Established 1845. | NEW YORK, MAY 4, 1889. | $3.00 A YEAR. Weekly.

1. Head on to sea at full speed. 2. Pilot house. 3. View aft at full speed. 4. Men's quarters, aft. 5. A sharp turn. 6. Helmsman platform. 7. The engine room. 8. The boiler room. 9. The galley. 10. 26 miles an hour.

OUR NEW NAVY—THE STILETTO RECONSTRUCTED AS A TORPEDO BOAT.—(From sketches made for Sci. Am. on special trial.)—[See p. 276.]

The Scientific American *weekly journal introduced its subscribers to the U.S. Navy's Wooden Torpedo Boat No. 1, the* Stiletto, *with this front-page illustration. (Courtesy* Scientific American.*)*

Four

The Requirements of a Seagoing Torpedo Boat

This chapter is from a dissertation by Assistant Naval Constructor H.G. Gillmor. It was read at the fifth general meeting of the Society of Naval Architects and Marine Engineers, held in New York on November 11 and 12, 1897. (See *Transactions,* edited by the secretary, Vol. V, 1897, pp. 57–64.)

It is imperative that the sea-going torpedo-boat [*sic*] shall be seaworthy—that is, capable of remaining safely at sea in all such weathers as may reasonably be anticipated. Since the size of the boat has so vital a bearing upon its efficiency, it is important to consider what limitations are placed upon size by the necessity of seaworthiness, in order that it may be determined whether the size of boat consistent with the other characteristics required is consistent with this demand.

Much is heard of the hardships of the crews of sea-going torpedo-boats and of the impossibility of their long sustaining the fatigue, etc., of the life. The remedy for this must lie in special training of men for this service. So long as the torpedo-boat is seaworthy, there can be no question of the possibility of men living sagely and comfortably on board, when once they have become accustomed to the life. It is to be expected that men whose service has been in ships of large displacement of in torpedo-boats in sheltered waters should be incapacitated when first they encounter unusually rough weather in torpedo-boats.

The size of sea-going torpedo-boats may then be fixed by the considerations as to the qualities which it is desirable to employ in its design, with the certainty that, due regard being had for stability, it may be made seaworthy and habitable so long as the vessel determined by these considerations is not less than 100' in length and 50 tons displacement. What are these qualities, what values do our needs assign to each, and what manner of boat is it to which a rational consideration of these will lead us?

The sea-going torpedo-boat must be prepared to perform two kinds of duty. It must be capable of making a torpedo attack upon the ships of the enemy, and must be prepared to stand guard over and protect from torpedo-boat attack the ships of its own side. To fill both these roles, it is necessary that it should possess the following features: 1. An efficient torpedo armament; 2. A gun armament sufficiently powerful for an attack upon other torpedo-boats; 3. High speed; 4. Sufficient coal capacity, and; 5. Good maneuvering qualities.

Torpedo boat destroyers of the battleship fleet in Portland Harbor, Oregon. Commonly called a destroyer, this large version of the torpedo boat was the principal protector of capital ships against enemy torpedo boats in the early 1900s. Since the onset of destroyer construction, this type of craft evolved from 105 tons to 1,200 tons.

Torpedo Armament

Torpedo experts are agreed that the long, 18" [Whitehead] torpedo is the most desirable for this purpose. There remains to be considered the number of tubes which should be installed. The bow tubes which were at one time generally fitted have been abandoned on account of the interference of the bow wave with the tube and on account of the high-speed boats running down the torpedo before it could gather way after being fired. Upon English, German, Italian, Russian, and our own first-class boats three training tubes have generally been installed. The Austrian, French, and Spanish boats of the same class, the English torpedo-boat destroyer and the German division-boat have but two each. There is very little experience upon which to base conclusions as to the necessary number of tubes. Provision for three torpedo-tubes with a torpedo for each, and for carrying two additional torpedoes, is in conformity with the views of the greater number of the progressive maritime powers.

The "gunners gang" aboard the Truxton *with the Mark I Whitehead torpedo.*

Gun Armament

The boat requires to be provided with an armament which will enable it to encounter and disable or turn back a boat attacking vessels over which guard is being kept. The 1-pounder gun has been shown to be incapable of stopping a torpedo-boat. The 3-pounder, possessing greater penetration and mining power, will. The guns and torpedoes will not generally be used at the same time. It is believed that three 3-pounder guns would make a battery which could be manned by the crew of the torpedo-boat, and which would be sufficiently powerful for the purpose.

Speed

High speed is necessary in the sea-going torpedo-boat to make it meet three important conditions. The first is that it shall be in a class by itself, capable of refusing engagement with vessels of any other class than its own. The second requires that it shall be capable of approaching and getting away, in a torpedo attack upon ships, with sufficient rapidity to make the attack a success. The third condition is that when standing guard over ships to protect them from the attacks of torpedo-boats it shall be capable of pursuing and engaging these boats. The speed of the fastest cruisers of the world, attained only by a very limited number, is 22 knots, so that a speed in excess of this is required in the sea-going torpedo-boat in order to meet the first condition. There seems reason to believe that the speed fixed by the first condition is not too low to be consistent with the second. The third condition requires a consideration of the boats with which our sea-going boats may be expected to contend. Of the

Launching a torpedo boat destroyer, Bath Iron Works, Bath, Maine.

more than sixteen hundred serviceable torpedo-boats which are now possessed, are building, or are projected by the nations of the world, that are but 260 having a speed of more than 25 knots. Of these, 153 are of the large size and high speed known in the English service as torpedo-boat destroyers, and 87 more are credited with a speed of but 26 knots. It is believed, therefore, that a speed of 26 knots would be sufficient to make our sea-going torpedo-boat capable of performing any service which is within her province. To produce the power necessary for this speed a single vertical engine possesses several advantages which recommend it for the purpose. It will require a smaller number of men to run it and keep it in order. The first cost of the single engine is very much less than that of two engines for the same power. The economy of the larger unit is superior to that of the smaller. The single engine admits of a roomier and more commodious engine-room than would be possible with a pair of engines in the same space.

Coal Capacity

Ideas vary widely as to the necessary coal capacity which should be given to a sea-going torpedo-boat. It is necessary that, when such boats are acting with a fleet, the embarrassment occasioned by the necessity of their procuring coal shall be reduced to the least possible, by giving them large a capacity as practicable and making some of the times of requiring coal by the torpedo-boat coincide with the times at which the larger ships of the fleet must seek coal. The normal endurance of our battleships of least endurance is about 7,000 nautical miles. It is not practicable to obtain so great a radius as this in the sea-going torpedo-boat. It is, however, possible to provide in the design of these boats for sufficient coal to steam 3,500 to 4,000 nautical miles at

Torpedo Boat Destroyer No. 8, the Lawrence. *The* Lawrence *had a length of 240 feet and a speed of 28.41 knots. Built by the Fore River Engine Company of East Braintree, Massachusetts, she was commissioned on April 14, 1903.*

Torpedo Boat Destroyer No. 16, the Worden. *The first* Worden *(No. 16) was laid down at Sparrows Point, Maryland, by the Maryland Steel Company and was launched on August 15, 1901. She was sponsored by Mrs. Daniel F. Worden, the daughter-in-law of Rear Admiral Worden, and was commissioned on St. Patrick's Day 1903, with Lt. Benjamin B. McCormick in command. (U.S. Navy records.)*

Torpedo Boat Destroyer No. 13, the Stewart. *The first* Stewart *was laid down on January 24, 1900, at Morris Heights, New York, by the Gas Engine and Power Company. She was launched on May 10, 1902, sponsored by Mrs. Paul Lee Cocke, granddaughter of Rear Admiral Stewart. She was commissioned on December 1, 1902, with Lt. Frederick A. Traut in command. (U.S. Navy records.)*

10 knots. The sea-going torpedo-boat would then require coal with the battleships of least endurance and once in each interval between the coaling of these ships. In connection with this matter of coal capacity the possibility of torpedo-boats receiving coal at sea from ships should be noted. In the voyage of the English torpedo-boats No. 61 and No. 62 . . . they received coal as they required it from the storeship Tyme, which accompanied them, the coaling being performed without great difficulty, even during some of the very rough weather which was encountered.

Maneuvering Qualities

The service required of the torpedo-boat demands that it should be capable of maneuvering easily in a small space. To offset the disadvantage in this regard which is brought in by the single screw proposed, the fitting of a bow rudder in addition to the usual stern rudder and for use in conjunction with it is suggested. This arrangement has been in satisfactory use upon boats constructed by Normand and Schichan for some years, and has proved satisfactory and productive of considerable improvement over maneuvering qualities of boats fitted with after rudders only.

A boat embodying the features which have been enumerated would, under the customary trial conditions with a load of 25 tons, representing the equipment, stores, coal, etc., on board, displace about 120 tons.

The principal dimensions are:

Torpedo-Boat Designs

Length on the water-line	141' 0"
Length over all	148' 5"
Maximum beam	15' 6"
Draft under screw	7' 6"
Displacement (trial)	127 tons
Speed	26 knots

A single four-cylinder triple expansion engine	Cylinders 20" X 29" X 30" and 30"
Stroke	18"
Revolutions, not more than	400
Indicated horse-power	2,700
Two water-tube boilers. Grate area, combined	110 sq. ft.
Coal capacity	40 tons

Machinery

Such a torpedo-boat could be constructed under the present industrial conditions for less than $100,000, so that at least two could be built for the cost of each of the largest of the boats which are now under construction for the Navy. In the design outlined in the sketch plans, the reserve of buoyancy is somewhat less than is commonly provided, although still more than 100 per cent of the displacement of the boat fully loaded. Provision is made for performing all the external service of the boat upon a platform which is raised some distance above the deck, so that, although the reserve of buoyancy and freeboard are slightly less, the height of the deck upon which service is performed is more than is commonly provided in sea-going torpedo-boats. It is believed that boats similar in type to the one indicated . . . would, with a well-trained crew, be fully capable of performing efficiently any duty which is within the province of the sea-going torpedo-boat.

Torpedo Boat Destroyer No. 57, the Tucker. *The first* Tucker *was laid down on November 9, 1914, at the Fore River Shipbuilding Company in Quincy, Massachusetts, and was launched on May 4, 1916. The boat was sponsored by Mrs. William Garty, the great-great-granddaughter of Capt. Samuel Tucker, and commissioned on April 11, 1916, with Lt. (jg) Frank Slingluff in temporary command until Lieutenant Commander Benysurd assumed command 13 days later.*

Prohibition of liquor, instituted by law on January 17, 1929, soon resulted in widespread smuggling of alcoholic beverages along the coastlines of the United States. The U.S. Department of the Treasury discovered that the Coast Guard simply did not have the ships to constitute a successful patrol. To cope with the problem, Pres. Calvin Coolidge authorized the transfer, in 1924, of 20 old destroyers, then in reserve and out of commission, from the navy to the Coast Guard.

On March 25, 1926, the Tucker *was activated and acquired by the Coast Guard, part of a second group of five to augment the original 20. Designated No. 23, she joined the "rum patrol" and chased rum runners, aiding in the attempt to enforce Prohibition laws.*

After Congress passed the Twenty-first Amendment to the Constitution to end Prohibition, the Tucker was returned to the navy on June 30, 1933. Her name was canceled on November 1, 1933, to free the name Tucker *for No. 374, and thereafter, the old destroyer was known by her hull designation, No. 57. For a time, No. 57 served as a sea scout training ship, docked at Sandy Hook, New Jersey. Struck from the navy list on October 24, 1936, No. 57 was sold on December 10, 1936, and reduced to a hulk two days before Christmas 1936. (U.S. Navy records.)*

Five
The Herreshoffs' Big Steel Torpedo Boats

Torpedo Boat No. 1, the *Cushing*

In 1887, the Herreshoff Manufacturing Company received its first contract from the U.S. Navy to build an all-steel torpedo boat. This vessel was designated by the navy as Seagoing Torpedo Boat No. 1 and was later christened USS *Cushing*. Representative of the group of armed vessels called the mosquito fleet, she was the first seagoing torpedo boat built in America.

The *Cushing* was lightly built, but most of her steel parts were electro-galvanized. Nathanael Herreshoff designed new and unusual engines for the *Cushing*. They were five-cylinder, quadruple-expansion engines with two low-pressure cylinders. If the valve gear had been between the cylinders, as in the usual engines, the engine would have been abnormally long, so he adopted the scheme of having the valves at the side of the cylinders and valves driven by a separate crankshaft—very much the same as today's internal combustion engines.

Bureau of Ordnance,
Navy Department
Washington City,
April 13th, 1888
[To] Commander C.F. Goodrich,
Inspector of Ordnance-in charge
Torpedo Station
Subject: Trial of Herreshoff boilers.

Sir:
A new Herreshoff boiler, specially designed for torpedo boat service and for use in Navy launches, has been installed in a boat belonging to the Herreshoff Manufacturing Company, at Bristol, R.I., and the company has asked the Department to have a Board witness certain trials with the boat, and to examine the boiler.

Please designate as the Board for the above purpose the following officers, viz.: Lieut. Comdr. G.A. Converse, Lieut. Karl Rohrer and Lieut. C. Mc.R. Winslow.

The Herreshoff Co. intends to make a comparative trial between the boat in which

Torpedo Boat No. 1, the Cushing, *is launched into Bristol Harbor on January 23, 1890.*

The Cushing *undergoes dock trials at the Herreshoff Manufacturing Company's boatyard in Bristol.*

their new boiler is installed and another boat similar in respects except that her boiler is of the ordinary Herreshoff type.

The Board is to witness these trials and to report results, with any other matters of interest that it may observe. A report is also to be made on the merits of the new boiler.

The trial is set for the 19th inst., and may continue for a few days.

Let the Board proceed to Bristol when necessary, in one of the cutters belonging to the Station, if convenient.

I am, Sir,
Your obedt. Servt.,
M. Sicard
Chief of Bureau

The following letter of report on the performance of the Herreshoff Manufacturing Company's new boiler is abbreviated from the original document, which is lengthy and technical.

Torpedo Station
Newport, R.I.
April 28, 1888
[To] Comdr. C.F. Goodrich, USN
Inspector of Ordnance in charge of
Torpedo Station

Sir,

In obedience to your order of the 16th instant requesting us as a board to proceed to Bristol, R.I. and witness certain trials with steam boilers designed by the Herreshoff Mfg. Co., . . . we have the honor to submit the following report.

The Herreshoff Mfg. Co. have constructed two boats identical in every aspect with the exception of the boilers. These boats are approximately sixty-five feet in length of eight tons displacement, are fitted with triple expansion engines and are designed for passenger service, that is they have great carrying capacity, and are not expected to make exceptionally high speed. One of these boats is fitted with the inducing Herreshoff coil boiler of the regular type; the other is fitted with a boiler of their invention which has not previously been tried.

The trials mapped out by the Herreshoff Mfg. Co. are as follows:

1. Efficiency of improved type of boiler on the natural craft.
2. Efficiency of improved boiler on the forced craft, i.e., steam jet.
3. Efficiency of old type of boiler on the natural craft.
4. Efficiency of old type of boiler on the forced craft.

We summarize the merits of the new boiler as follows:

1. The economic qualities do not differ essentially from those of the other boilers of the water circulator type.

> 2. Using a defined water level is a decided advantage as it enables the furnace to produce steam of uniform quality—i.e. prevents its superheating it, or carrying a surplus of water to the engine.
> 3. From the nature of its construction the boiler can be easily and quickly repaired.
> 4. The boiler which we saw in operation weighed but 2950 lb., and developed, in connection with the triple expansion engine used slightly upwards of 45HP. We consider it extremely light for the power developed, a feature which especially commends it for use in torpedo boats and service launches.
> 5. Steam can be generated in a very short time [and] a pressure of 120 lb. was obtained in less than 15 minutes, without making any effort for time. When running with natural craft the pressure was increased by the use of a steam jet from 120lb. to 180lb. in less than five minutes, and was maintained at the higher pressure.
> 6. The external shell of the boiler was cool to the touch, the heat developed being entirely absorbed within. A feature which must be of great importance in a closed, confined fire room. The only objectionable feature which at present suggests itself consists in the numerous joints in the structure. In the boiler tried, the joints gave no trouble whatever, and we see no reason why they should if made with due care.
>
> The desirability of this boiler can, in our opinion, only be determined by experience.
>
> We consider these trials of this boiler, and also the engine—triple expansion type—to have been thoroughly successful in every respect.
>
> Very respectfully submitted
> George A. Converse, Lt Comdr. US Navy
> Karl Rohrer, Lieut. US Navy
> C. Mc. R. Winslow Lieut. US Navy

The *Cushing*'s two engines did not develop as much power as was expected (800 horsepower per engine), so she only exceeded her contract speed by about half a knot. The *Cushing* was built for a cost of $82,750. At that time, the U.S. Navy Department would award premiums of $2,000 and more for each quarter of a knot in excess of 24 knots. A penalty of $4,000 would be deducted from the contract price if the speed of the boat fell below 22 knots. Speed trials consisted of a continuous run of three hours, during which time the boat had to attain a mean speed of 22 knots.

Some 140 feet long, 15 feet 1 inch abeam, and 4 feet 10 inches in draft, the *Cushing* displaced 116,000 pounds. Her top speed was 23 knots. Her armament consisted of three rapid-firing 6-pound Hotchkiss breech-loading rifles, two or more Gatling guns, and three torpedo tubes. The torpedo room was located under the "whale back" on the bow

The Cushing *undergoes a navy inspection in dry dock before being fitted with her armament.*

and consisted of two partly enclosed tubes. The loading of torpedoes, the charging of the launching tubes, and the handling of the breech mechanism were conducted in this compartment. The third torpedo launching tube was deck-mounted aft. The torpedoes could be fired from the bow tubes while the boat was moving at top speed, using an electrical device held in the hand of the commander in the conning tower. Her complement was 20 enlisted men and two officers.

The *Cushing* was launched into Bristol Harbor on January 23, 1890. Her sponsor was Kitty B. Herreshoff, and the *Bristol Phoenix* carried this story of the event:

> THE SEA-GOING TORPEDO BOAT CUSHING—which it was intended to launch from the Herreshoff Manufacturing Co.'s yard Wednesday morning, but owing to the very heavy wind which then prevailed was necessarily postponed—was successfully launched about 9:45 o'clock Thursday morning in the presence of a large gathering of spectators.
>
> As the handsome craft glided gracefully from the ways to the water, loud, long and hearty cheers rent the air. Miss Kitty Herreshoff broke a bottle of wine over the bow at the christening.
>
> Admiral Luce stood at the *Cushing*'s stern and seemed to enjoy the occasion heartily. A more successful launch was never witnessed. Among the visitors present were Admiral Luce, U.S.N.; Commander Converse, U.S.N.; Lieutenant Winslow, U.S.N.; Major Livermore, U.S.A.; Captain James Lawless and Col. M.T. Bennett, of this town, and many others.[6]

As the first torpedo boat built for the U.S. Navy, the *Cushing* was attached to the Squadron

The Cushing *hauled out sometime before before 1898. This view of the* Cushing *affords an excellent view of the boat's odd-shaped screws.*

The Cushing *in lifeboat rescue exercises.*

The Cushing *at pier side, November 1900. The* Cushing *is shown with a new coat of dark night camouflage paint. Her decks are now cluttered with gear, her deck-mounted starboard torpedo launching tube is visible, and her small guns are shrouded. At this late date, the* Cushing *still retains the distinctively sleek curve of her bow. (U.S. Navy photograph.)*

The Cushing, *1903. In this view of the fully armed* Cushing, *her three 1-pound rapid-fire guns and two deck-mounted torpedo tubes are clearly visible. The once sleek beauty of the* Cushing's *bow has been transformed into a stub-nosed affair to accommodate the enclosed torpedo tube. (Photograph by F.M. Child.)*

The Cushing, *1888. The government's first all-steel, seagoing torpedo boat, at 105-feet* Cushing *was only slightly larger than the* Stiletto. *She obtained a maximum speed of 24 knots.*

of Evolution and was equipped for experimental work to complete the development of torpedo outfits and to gather data for the service. Her first commander was Lt. C.M. Winslow. Commissioning ceremonies were held on April 22, 1890. In July, the local press made the following report about the *Cushing:*

> THE UNITED STATES TORPEDO BOAT CUSHING, built by the Herreshoff Manufacturing Co., of this town, made a remarkably fast run of 120 miles from New York to New London, Friday afternoon of last week.
>
> She ran at the marvelously quick time of 4 hours, 42 minutes and 45 seconds. The *Cushing* lay at anchor Sunday at New London but sailed for Newport on Monday morning. There she will be fitted with everything pertaining to a torpedo boat.

On September 8, 1891, she reported for duty at the Naval Torpedo Station at Newport. Except for a brief period out of commission (November 11, 1891, to January 11, 1892), the *Cushing* continued her torpedo experiments in the waters of Narragansett Bay until 1893.

The *Cushing* arrived at Hampton Roads, Virginia, on March 31, 1893, for temporary duty with the U.S. Naval Review Fleet and, in April, she escorted HMS *Blake* and HMS *Caravels* to New York. The *Cushing* returned to duty at Newport on May 6, working with the Whitehead torpedo. Based in Key West, Florida, beginning on December 31, 1897, the *Cushing* reported to the North Atlantic Fleet's blockading force for picket patrol in the Florida Straits and courier duty for the force. On February 11, 1898, while making a passage to Havana, the *Cushing* lost Ens. J.C. Breckinridge overboard in heavy seas. For their heroic efforts to save him, gunner's mate J. Everetts and ship's cook D. Atkins were awarded the Medal of Honor.

With the declaration of war between the United States and Spain, the *Cushing* was assigned to patrol the Cays. On August 7, 1898, she captured four small vessels and towed them to her anchorage at Piedras Cay. Four days later, armed boats from the *Cushing* and *Gwin* (another Herreshoff-built torpedo boat) captured and burned a 20-ton Spanish schooner.

The torpedo room of the Cushing. *A second enclosed torpedo tube was added to the* Cushing*'s armament, in her bow, below the waterline. This interior view is representative of the torpedo launching machinery on all early U.S. Navy torpedo boats. In the foreground is an 18-inch Whitehead torpedo in readiness for launching.*

Keeping the blockade. The flagship New York *signals orders off Havana. In this improbable scenario, the artist has depicted the* Cushing *with her bow torpedo tube installed during the Spanish-American War (1898). This hardware, however, was not in place until after November 1900. (From* Leslie's Official History of the Spanish-American War.*)*

Returning north later in August 1898, the *Cushing* resumed her operations at the Naval Torpedo Station at Newport until she was decommissioned on November 8, 1898. From 1901 to 1911, she was attached to the U.S. Reserve Torpedo Flotilla at Norfolk and was sunk on September 24, 1920, after being used as a target.

THE *PORTER* AND THE *DUPONT*

The following is an undated draft of a letter to the secretary of the navy or the Bureau of Construction and Repair. It was prepared by Comdr. George A. Converse, who was the inspector of the torpedo boats and was stationed at the Newport torpedo station.

> Sir:
>
> 1. Paragraph 1, General Description of Torpedo Boats, Nos. 5, 6, and 7, and also the general plan of these boats submitted by us contemplate the installment of triple expansion engines, having four cylinders placed one abaft the other in a fore and aft line, in the same horizontal plane.
>
> 2. We have recently designed, with a view to their being used in these vessels a new type of triple expansion engines, having the same general characteristics as that above named, but differing in that the forward and after cylinders are placed above and overlap by nearly one-half their diameters the two other cylinders. By this arrangement the following advantages are gained:
>
> > (a) The cylinders are arranged in pairs; and each pair connects to two cranks placed 180° from each other, and having no intermediate bearing. The piston rods and connecting rods of each pair of cylinders thus balance each other, and shocks caused by overcoming the inertia of these parts are practically annihilated.
> >
> > (b) The length of the engine is materially decreased and the pairs of cranks, being brought close together, reduce the vertical couple tending to produce vibration to a minimum—a result greatly to be desired.

The Porter *cruising at moderate speed. The* Porter *distinguished herself during the Spanish-American War.*

The Porter *in dry dock at Brooklyn.*

(c) The length of the new engines being ___ feet ___ inches less than originally proposed, leaves available space which can be utilized to great advantage for other purposes.

3. We therefore respectfully request, in accordance with the provisions of the 11th clause, and under the conditions of the 2nd clause of our Contract, that we may be allowed to substitute this type of engine for the original design, and estimate that the cost of such change will not exceed $ ___.

4. Blue print of the proposed engine is transmitted herewith.

Very respectfully,

Torpedo Station,
Newport, R.I.,
Nov. 4th, 1895.
[To] Judge Advocate General,
Navy Department,
Washington, D.C.

My Dear Lemly:
I have delayed furnishing you with an abstract of the points which should be covered by the instructions to be issued to me as General Inspector of Torpedo Boats Nos.

The McKenzie *(left) and the* Porter *in formation for a practice torpedo run.*

6 and 7 until I shall have received and have had a chance to examine carefully the specifications for machinery for these boats.

I believe they are, in their general nature very similar to the specifications for the hulls and in the latter I find that there are several points which would be well to have covered by my instructions.

I have made frequent visits to Bristol in the Cushing and am glad to report that matters are progressing satisfactorily, and that the outlook is, in my opinion, most promising. Designer N.G. Herreshoff has taken up the matter with a great deal of interest and is devoting all of his time to it. About ten days ago I was present at some experiments which he conducted in towing models at different speeds for determining the resistance of various forms of hulls, and the one selected for the torpedo boat gave by far the most satisfactory results. From the data then obtained he is personally constructing, and has nearly finished, a half-model of the boat, some six feet in length, from which the off-sets for bending the frames will be taken, and the development of the hull-plating made.

The Porter. *At 180 feet, the* Porter *was considerably larger than the* Cushing; *she cost $147, 000 to build and made a record speed of 27.5 knots.*

Three draughtsmen are now at work on the detail drawings of the main engines, which promise to be a novelty in their line, and to embrace the good points of the Cushing's engines and such improvements as have been developed by Thornycroft and Normand in their recent boats, particularly the *Forban,* which a few weeks ago attained such remarkable speed.

Orders for bulb angles and shapers for the hull framing have been placed, and some of the material is expected by the 20th of this month.

Of course there will be little to make an official report upon for some time yet; but I can only state that, personally, I am much gratified at the condition of affairs.

Very truly yours,
G.A. Converse,
Commander, U.S.N.

The war with Spain was on the horizon when, in the fall of 1895, the Herreshoff Manufacturing Company accepted two contracts from the U.S. Navy to design and build two steel-hulled torpedo boats: the USS *Porter* and the USS *Dupont.*

The design of these vessels—boilers, engines, and all—required the special inventiveness of Nathanael Herreshoff. Both boats were double-enders at the waterline and below. They were good sea boats and made exceptional speed—both about 31 knots.

As is frequently the case today, cost overruns on government contracts were common, and the *Porter* and *Dupont* cost more to build than their contract price. Fortunately for the Herreshoff boatyard, the U.S. Navy Department at that time gave substantial bonuses for each quarter of a knot that a vessel exceeded her contract speed. As both boats did exceed their contract speed, the large bonuses awarded to the Herreshoff Manufacturing Company offset the yard's cost overruns.

At that time, one of the great difficulties in many torpedo boats throughout the world was vibration from what were then considered high-speed engines. The usual torpedo boat engine was quite long because it had valves between the cylinders and, although the whole mass of moving parts could be somewhat counterbalanced, the ends of these engines gyrated considerably around the center of weight. In fact, the vibration trouble of the reciprocating engine brought about the turbine, and before the reduction gear was

The Porter*'s armament consisted of four 1-pound rapid-fire guns and three 18-inch Whitehead torpedo tubes.*

The Porter *pours on the steam on her trial trip. (Period postcard.)*

used, the turbine itself had serious propeller vibration problems.

For the *Porter* and *Dupont,* Nathanael Herreshoff designed remarkable engines that were almost completely balanced both statically and dynamically. They were four-cylinder, triple-expansion engines with two of the cylinders above so that, together with valves and valve gear at the side, the overall length of the engines was less than half that of other engines of their class and horsepower. Because the two endcrank throws were opposite each other, the pistons and reciprocating parts counterbalanced each other.

The moving parts were extremely light; the crankshaft was hollow at both the main bearings and the crankpins. Each engine weighed 18,750 pounds and developed about

The Porter *in dry dock at the Brooklyn Navy Yard. (Courtesy* Scientific American.*)*

The Porter *(pictured) and her sister, the* Dupont, *were the largest of the Herreshoff-built U.S. Navy torpedo boats. The* Porter, *commissioned in 1897, was discarded in 1912. During the construction of these boats, naval inspectors so infuriated the Herreshoff brothers that they resolved never to tender for navy contracts after delivering the boats currently under construction. The firm survived many decades into the 20th century, filling the needs of the luxury steam and the sail yacht market. (Courtesy* Scientific American.*)*

1,700 horsepower. It is noteworthy that these engines were so well engineered and built that they gave some 20 years of service without the need for any major repairs.

The *Porter* and *Dupont* each had three boilers, and the boilers had grate areas of 53.5 feet, with heating surfaces of 2,710 feet. They carried a boiler pressure of only a little more than 200 pounds, and it seems remarkable today that these torpedo boats made such great speed, considering that boiler pressures of over 1,000 pounds are quite common today. They carried about 20 tons of coal and other naval equipment on their trial runs, and they had bunker capacity for 60 tons.

Torpedo Station,
Newport, R.I
Jan. 6th, 1896.
[To] Herreshoff Manufacturing Co.,
Bristol, R.I.

Gentlemen:
I enclose herewith drafts of two letters, one relating to the proposed change in engines, and the other in boilers for the torpedo boats Nos. 6 and 7.

In my opinion it will be best to have each accompanied by a blue print of the same relative size and general character as those submitted with the original specifications, in order that the Navy Department may be able to make comparisons.

I will prepare a third letter in regard to the modifications of the hulls which is

> caused by the proposed changes in engines and boilers, and forward it to you probably by tomorrow's mail.
>
> I started for Bristol in the *Stiletto* Saturday A.M., but encountered a very rough sea of Sandy Point, and the boat being covered with ice I deemed it better to return without proceeding and trying to effect a landing, about which there was some doubt. As soon as the weather moderates, I will be up to see you.
>
> Very truly yours,
> G.A. Converse, Commander, U.S.N.
> General Inspector Torpedo boats, Nos. 6 & 7.

The first *Porter* (Torpedo Boat No. 6) measured 175 feet 6 inches long with a beam of 17 feet 9 inches and a draft of 4 feet 8 inches. She was capable of a top speed of 29 knots, and her armament included four 1-pound guns and three 18-inch torpedo tubes.

The *Porter* was laid down in February 1896 and launched on September 9, 1896. She was sponsored by Agnes M. Herreshoff and commissioned on February 20, 1897, at Newport.

With Lt. John Charles Fremont as her first commander, the *Porter* sailed to Washington, D.C., on February 27, 1897, for inspection, and in March, the vessel was further examined at New York by the chief of the Bureau of Navigation. She operated between New London and Newport. She then visited New York from July 15 to October 3 before getting under way for her winter port, Charleston, South Carolina. The *Porter* cruised in the southern waters until December 8 and then proceeded to Key West, where she was stationed for the month of January 1898.

Shortly after the *Porter* arrived at Mobile, Alabama, on January 26, 1898, for a visit, she was ordered to return to Key West for the blockade of Cuba. When the United States declared war on Spain, she was already patrolling the waters off Key West and the Dry Tortugas. The *Porter* returned to Key West on March 22 for replenishment.

On April 22, 1898, the *Porter* departed Key West with the North Atlantic Fleet for the blockade of the north coast of Cuba. She soon made contact with the enemy, capturing two Spanish schooners, the *Sofia* and *Matielda,* on April 23 and 24. After refueling at Key West, she resumed blockade duty off Cape Haitien, Haiti, keeping a watchful eye out for the Spanish squadron. She participated in the three-hour bombardment of San Juan on May 12–13 with the nine ships of Rear Adm. W.T. Sampson's fleet. During the attack, the *Porter* maintained a close position under the batteries with the *Detroit* but was not hit.

The *Porter* returned on May 13–14, 1898, to the blockade of the north coast of Hispaniola, cruising off Samana Bay, Santo Domingo, and Porto Plata, Haiti. After a brief interval at Key West and Mobile (May 18–25), she joined Commodore Schley's squadron off Santiago, Cuba, and helped bottle up the elusive Spanish warships. While silencing the shore batteries, the *Porter* came under heavy fire on June 7 but was undamaged. Later, between June 11 and June 17, she supported the Marine beachhead at Guantanamo Bay. Then, taking up her station off Santiago on June 17 and again on June 21–22, she bombarded Socapa battery until early July, when she left for New York via Key West.

The Porter *on the Hudson, with Grant's tomb in the background. (Period stereo view card.)*

Her fighting days over, the *Porter* arrived at the New York yard on July 9, 1898, was placed in reduced commission, and was decommissioned on November 5 of that year. She was recommissioned on October 10, 1899, at New York to serve as a training ship for firemen at Newport, Norfolk, and Annapolis. She was put in reserve commission in late 1901 with the U.S. Reserve Torpedo Flotilla and continued her duty through 1907.

A valued resource, the *Porter* was once more recommissioned on January 31, 1907, and was ordered to Pensacola on February 21. As flagship of the 3rd Torpedo Flotilla, she engaged in torpedo runs in St. Joseph's Bay, Florida, from March 4 to April 22.

The *Porter* acted as naval escort to the remains of Gov. DeWitt Clinton in New York Harbor on May 29, 1908, before returning on July 1 to the U.S. Reserve Torpedo Flotilla at Norfolk.

The *Porter* was commissioned a fourth time on May 14, 1909, at Charleston, South Carolina. With Lt. Harold R. Stark in command, she was assigned to the 3rd Division,

Atlantic Torpedo Flotilla. She proceeded to Provincetown, Massachusetts, on June 10, 1909, for fleet exercises that lasted until August 5. She departed there on August 29 for Hampton Roads and the Southern Drill Grounds, later joining the fleet at New York for the Hudson-Fulton Celebration on October 1. She was reassigned on November 14 to the U.S. Reserve Torpedo Flotilla at Charleston, where she remained until October 1911.

The *Porter* sailed again on October 30, 1911, for New York, where she took part in the fleet naval review on November 2 for Pres. Theodore Roosevelt. The President had ordered the mobilization "to test the preparedness of the fleet and the efficiency of our organization on the ships in the yards." Afterward, the *Porter* returned to the U.S. Reserve Torpedo Flotilla at Philadelphia. She was mobilized in October 1912 for yet another review at New York, which was inspected by the President on October 15. In November 1912, the *Porter* was struck from the navy list of ships and was sold to Andrew Olsen on December 30, 1912, at New York.

The first *Dupont* (Torpedo Boat No. 7) was launched on March 30, 1897, and was sponsored by a Miss L. Converse. The *Dupont* was commissioned on September 23, with Lt. (jg) S.S. Wood as commander.

The *Dupont* was 176 feet 6 inches long and 17 feet 9 inches abeam. She had a draft of 4 feet 8 inches and a displacement of 165,000 pounds, with a top speed of 28 knots. Armament included four 1-pound guns and three 18-inch torpedo tubes.

The *Dupont* operated on the East Coast, carrying dispatches and training naval reservists until the outbreak of the Spanish-American War. She carried orders and messages to ships lying at the Dry Tortugas and Key West, and served on picket and patrol duty off Key West, Matanzas, and Santiago, Cuba.

To illustrate the spirit of the *Dupont*'s men, Commo. Winfield S. Schley, commander of the American squadron laying off Cienfuegos, wrote on May 22, 1898, that the *Dupont*—having started for Key West to repair a hole she had in her hull from bumping a coral reef—read the signals ordering the squadron to Santiago. The *Dupont* came rushing back to beg permission to go along; a plug would keep the water from flooding the boat well enough if a fight with Cervera was in prospect.

The Dupont, *with a hole in her bottom, rushes at full speed to join Commodore Schiley's squadron at Santiago.*

The Dupont *in dry dock. A* Scientific American *report reads: "A very excellent view is here afforded of one of our hornets of the sea, the vixenish 'Dupont,' which is one of the two largest torpedo boats in the present American Navy. This vessel, which is 175 feet in length, and seventeen in breadth, is here fully exposed, so that her hull appearance is clearly visible. She is just completed, and is credited with a speed of 27.5 knots, and though five feet longer than the 'Rowan,' her displacement is two tons less, and her speed is nearly two knots greater. Four other torpedo boats, viz., the 'Goldsborough,' to be of 247 tons displacement, the 'Farragut,' of 273 tons, the 'Bailey,' of 235 tons, and the 'Stringham,' of 340 tons, are now building, so that the torpedo fleet now completed under construction will number 22 fast flying boats, a few of which will be classed among the most powerful in the world. Of these, the 'Stiletto,' of wood, with 359 horse power, is smallest, and the 'Stringham,' of steel, with 7200 horse power, will be the largest. The navy bill, passed in April, provides for the construction of 28 additional torpedo craft, 16 destroyers and 12 torpedo boats, the former to cost $295, 000, and the latter $170,000 each, but these will not be completed before August, 1899." (Courtesy* Scientific American.*)*

The Dupont *and the* Ericsson *in the New York Navy Yard dry dock. The 165-ton, Herreshoff-built* Dupont *is shown in the foreground, with the 120-ton* Ericsson *in the background. At the time of this 1898 photograph, the* Dupont *and the* Porter *were the largest torpedo boats in the American navy. They were modeled after the sleek racing lines of the Herreshoff Manufacturing Company's earlier sport-racing craft.*

The Dupont *floating free in the flooded dry dock, 1898. (Postcard by E. Muller.)*

The Dupont *in a 1909 navy parade, North River, New York.*

The *Dupont* returned to New York on August 9, 1898. Arriving at Newport, Rhode Island, on November 4, 1898, she was placed out of commission four days later. She remained at Newport out of commission but was employed occasionally in experimental and training duty. From 1901 to 1909, she was based at Norfolk in the U.S. Reserve Torpedo Flotilla. During this time, she was recommissioned twice. From September 1903 to September 1904, she was used as a training ship at the U.S. Naval Academy and, from June 1905 to June 1906, was engaged in operations with the Coast Squadron on the Atlantic Coast and in the Gulf of Mexico.

Recommissioned again on May 14, 1909, the *Dupont* cruised along the coast with the Atlantic torpedo fleet until placed in reserve again at the Charleston Navy Yard in November 1909. From May 1910 to June 1911, she served the naval militia of North Carolina and, after lying in Newport from October 1911 to May 1914, she was loaned to the Massachusetts Naval Militia on June 10, 1914.

With the entry of the United States into World War I, the *Dupont* was recommissioned on April 9, 1917, and was assigned to duty in the Second Naval District. The following year, she was attached to the Coast Patrol Squadron, New London Station, for duty in Narragansett Bay. Beginning on August 1, 1918, she was known as Coast Torpedo Boat No. 3, thus releasing the name *Dupont* for new construction. She arrived at the Philadelphia Navy Yard on January 24, 1919, and was decommissioned there on March 8, 1919. She was sold on July 19, 1920.

THE *TALBOT,* THE *GWIN,* AND THE *MORRIS*

In 1897, the Herreshoffs built U.S. Navy Torpedo Boat No. 14, the *Morris,* as well as the *Talbot* and *Gwin* (Nos. 15 and 16, respectively). The *Morris* was 140 feet long, and the *Gwin*

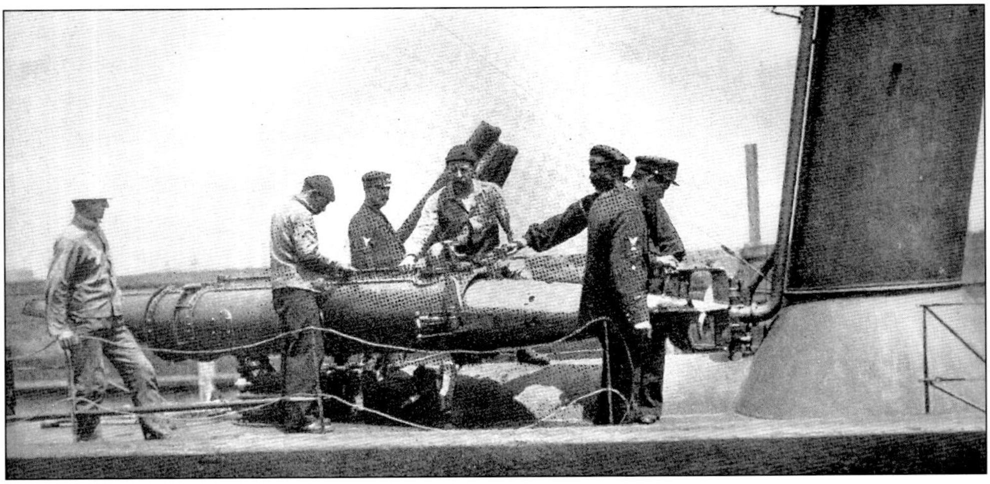

A deck tube of the Talbot *and an 18-inch Whitehead torpedo. (Courtesy* Collier's Weekly.*)*

The Talbot, c. *1906. The* Talbot *fires a Whitehead Mark III broadside from her mooring at the Naval Torpedo Station at Newport. (NTS photograph.)*

The Talbot. *Although she was built for use as a home coast defense torpedo boat, the* Talbot *was pressed into service on the coast of Cuba during the Spanish-American War.*

and *Talbot* measured almost 100 feet long each.

The first *Talbot* (Torpedo Boat No. 15) was 99 feet 6 inches long, 12 feet 6 inches abeam, and drew 3 feet 3 inches, with a displacement of 46.5 tons. Her top speed was 21.5 knots. Included in her armament were two 18-inch torpedo tubes. The *Talbot*'s hull was laid down on April 8, 1897. She was launched on November 14, 1897, and commissioned on April 4, 1898. Her first commander was Lt. (jg) William R. Shoemaker.

The *Talbot* cruised the East Coast, making calls in Maryland, Virginia, and North Carolina before arriving at Havana, Cuba, on August 2, 1898. She reported to the flagship and received mail for the blockading squadron. At nine that evening, while en route to Key West for coal, she sighted the dark hull of a ship off the port bow. The *Talbot* signaled and stopped her engines but was rammed by the tug *Uncus.* The bow of the tug penetrated a foot into the torpedo boat's coal bunker, bending in two frames and crushing the side plating to below the waterline. The tug towed the *Talbot* to Piedras Cay, where temporary repairs were made the next day to enable the damaged ship to proceed to Key West.

The *Talbot* reached Key West on August 5, 1898, and got under way 10 days later for New York. She arrived at the New York Navy Yard on September 6 and was made ready for sea again in early October. She was then assigned to the U.S. Naval Academy for duty supporting midshipmen training, mooring at Annapolis. On June 11, 1899, the *Talbot* moved to Norfolk to participate in a one-year evaluation of experimental fuel oils. At the completion of this test program, she resumed her duties at the academy.

The *Talbot* was decommissioned on February 20, 1904, and was attached to the U.S. Reserve Torpedo Flotilla at Norfolk. She was recommissioned on August 31, 1906, and assigned to special duty between Norfolk and Annapolis. From early 1908 to September

Completed in 1898, the Talbot *was one of the last of the Herreshoff torpedo boats built for the U.S. Navy. The* Talbot *model was used in 1917 as a basis for exploratory designs for a new 105-foot class submarine chaser. She displaced 52 to 58 tons and had a speed of 19 knots. (U.S. Navy photograph.)*

The Talbot *in New York, 1900. The 46-ton* Talbot, *shown with her armament shrouded, proved to be too small and slow for effective torpedo boat service in the late war. (U.S. Navy photograph.)*

The Gwin *and the* Talbot, *1898. Shown under construction in the Herreshoff boatyard, the* Gwin *and the* Talbot *were the smallest in their class. (U.S. Navy photograph.)*

1911, she served at the Naval Torpedo Station at Newport. On October 22, 1911, the *Talbot* was reassigned to Indian Head, Maryland, for service as a tender. Before assuming her new duty, she proceeded to Norfolk for her annual inspection and was found unfit for further naval use.

The *Talbot* was inactivated on May 1, 1912, but was retained "in service" as a ferryboat to be operated between the Washington Navy Yard and the naval facilities at Indian Head. In April 1918, the *Talbot* was renamed the *Berceau* and reclassified as a ferryboat. On July 17, 1920, she was designated Yard Ferry Boat No. 3. She remained on ferry duty until June 18, 1940, when she was placed out of service and towed to Philadelphia. The *Berceau* was struck from the navy list of ships on July 18, 1944, and sold for scrap.

The first *Gwin* (Torpedo Boat No. 16) was launched on November 15, 1897. Her length was 100 feet; her beam, 12 feet 6 inches; and her draft, 3 feet 3 inches. Her top speed was 20 knots. The *Gwin* was commissioned at Newport on April 4, 1898, with Lt. (jg) C.S. Williams as her first commander. She departed Newport on June 24, 1898, cruising down the eastern seaboard as far as Florida, and then patrolled off Cuba between August 6 and 14, 1898, as America went to war with Spain. She returned north to Annapolis on August 31 and served as a cadet training ship for the U.S. Naval Academy until placed in reserve at Norfolk on July 10, 1903.

The fully armed Gwin *under way in Narragansett Bay. (NTS photograph.)*

The Cyane, *previously known as the* Gwin, *is shown in January 1922 after accidentally ramming the seawall while coming into the Naval Torpedo Station at Newport. The ship was repaired by naval personnel by early March 1922 and soon returned to duty. (NTS photograph.)*

Torpedo carriage and torpedo tube on a typical U.S. Navy torpedo boat, c. *1900.*

The *Gwin* remained in reserve until June 1908, when she began assisting in experimental torpedo work at the Newport torpedo station. This duty ended on April 18, 1914, when the *Gwin* was decommissioned for use as a ferryboat. On April 11, 1918, her name was changed to *Cyane,* and she was reclassified as Yard Ferry Boat No. 4 on July 17, 1920. Her name was struck from the navy list of ships on April 30, 1924, and she was sold for scrap on September 24, 1925.

The *Morris* (Torpedo Boat No. 14) was the fifth U.S. Navy boat to be named *Morris* since August 1779. Torpedo Boat No. 14 was laid down at the Herreshoff yard on November 19, 1897. At 140 feet in length, she displaced 105 tons and carried three 18-inch torpedo tubes. She was launched on April 18, 1898, and commissioned on May 11, 1898, at Newport, with Lt. C.E. Fox in command.

After an East Coast shakedown cruise, the *Morris* arrived in Narragansett Bay at Newport for torpedo range tender services at the torpedo station on Goat Island. She remained in Newport until World War I, when she began patrol duties. From April 19, 1918, through early March 1919, she patrolled the West Indies, investigating suspected enemy sabotage. With her name changed to Torpedo Boat No. 6, she returned to Newport and was decommissioned on March 24, 1919, but served as a torpedo range tender in Newport for five years. The last of the old torpedo boats, she was struck from the naval register on January 24, 1924, and was sold at public auction on October 10, 1924, to Frank B. Jones of Wilmington, Delaware.

The Morris *under way in Narragansett Bay. The* Morris *successfully operated throughout her career as an experimental and training platform for launching torpedoes at the Newport torpedo station. (Period postcard.)*

Firing a torpedo. The Morris *fires a Whitehead torpedo broadside while under way. (Period postcard.)*

Six

The Herreshoff Legacy

In 1895, the U.S. Navy Department decided to have several torpedo boats built. Only those manufactured in Bristol were of Herreshoff design; all the others were navy-designed vessels. Despite all their ingenious and innovative hulls and engines, the Herreshoff brothers lacked tact. This, combined with an impatience with the U.S. military bureaucracy, brought an end to the Herreshoff Manufacturing Company's government contracts.

The Herreshoffs had to deal with difficult political appointees and civil servants, some of whom had very little training in the finer points of marine engineering but were required to pass judgment on the Herreshoff boats.

Some of the navy's marine inspectors caused annoyance to the Herreshoff Manufacturing Company. During construction of the *Dupont,* for example, navy inspectors condemned the boat's engine piston rod guides, saying they were made of the wrong kind of steel. Nathanael Herreshoff, his experience in such matters notwithstanding, gave in on the matter and made new piston guides according to the government specifications. The new guides were installed in the *Dupont*'s four engines and, shortly into her trial run, the new guide rods heated up so badly that she could not run well. Upon returning to the yard, Herreshoff asked for and received permission to temporarily reinstall the original guide rods in order to complete the trials, which were conducted without further mishap.

L. Francis Herreshoff later wrote in his book about Nathanael Herreshoff that "Captain Nat" and John Herreshoff were so mad about the incident that they shook hands in the office and agreed not to build any more vessels for the U.S. Navy Department after they finished their present contracts.[7]

At the very moment that the brothers were agreeing to quit bidding on government contracts, they were studying U.S. Navy plans and preparing bids for the construction of at least one torpedo boat and a light-draft gunboat. U.S. Navy Department blueprints, drawn and supplied by the Bureau of Construction and Repair to the Herreshoff Manufacturing Company, were saved by a longtime Herreshoff employee. These blueprints were salvaged and are today preserved at the Naval War College Museum in Newport. The existence of these plans was brought to the attention of the author by native Bristolian Frank Puniello, who later donated them to the Naval War College Museum. The plans that include engine specifications for the torpedo boats Nos. 24 through 35 are dated July 14, 1898. Boat No. 24, which was eventually built by the Bath Iron Works, was commissioned on October 18, 1901, as the *Bagley.*

One may speculate as to how the Bristol waterfront would have developed had the U.S. Navy become the Herreshoffs' major employer in the World War II era. There can be no doubt that the Herreshoff Manufacturing Company would have been a prime contractor, building fleets of the navy's wooden-hulled patrol torpedo (PT) boats. During the 1940s,

Firing a Whitehead torpedo, 1904. An experimental Whitehead Mark III torpedo is fired from the Newport torpedo station's east dock. The Talbot *(Torpedo Boat No. 15) is visible in the background. (Photograph by R.G. Skerrett.)*

"Governors of several states watching Torpedo Flotilla Review at Newport, Rhode Island." (Period photo postcard by Underwood & Underwood.)

The Morris *at the Naval Torpedo Station at Newport, Goat Island. (NTS photograph.)*

PT boats were armed with weapons made at the Newport torpedo station, berthed at Melville (Portsmouth), Rhode Island, and crews trained in Narragansett Bay.

Although the Herreshoffs' government work came to a premature and rather distasteful end, their contributions to naval architecture and their influence on later torpedo developments were much more long-lived. With their innovations and daring, the Herreshoffs of Bristol revolutionized the design and performance of the late-19th-century torpedo boat. And, perhaps of equal importance, the Herreshoff torpedo boats played major roles in later submarine torpedo developments at the Naval Torpedo Station at Newport.

Blue jackets aboard the Morris *demonstrate how to load a Whitehead torpedo. (Period postcard.)*

The torpedo boat Bagley *(Torpedo Boat No. 24) at Annapolis, Maryland. The first Bagley was launched on September 26, 1900, by Bath Iron Works of Bath, Maine. She was sponsored by Mrs. Josephus Daniels, sister of Ens. Worth Bagley, and was commissioned on October 18, 1901, with Ens. W.M. Dowell in command. The* Bagley *operated along the East Coast until going into reserve at Norfolk Navy Yard on February 19, 1903. On September 14, 1907, she was placed in full commission and reported to the Naval Academy. She remained on duty at the academy until March 13, 1914, when she was placed in reserve at Annapolis. Recommissioned on March 29, 1917, the* Bagley *was fitted out at New York and attached to the Harbor Entrance Patrol Third Naval District. On August 1, 1918, the* Bagley *was redesignated and renamed Coast Torpedo Boat No. 10. She operated from the marine base in Brooklyn. Her duties of patrolling, scouting ahead of the convoys leaving harbor, and escorting were continuous until she was decommissioned on March 12, 1919. (U.S. Navy records.)*

As the concept of self-propelled torpedoes caught on with U.S. inventors near the turn of the century, Herreshoff boats were involved in the trials and testing of the experimental weapons. The *Stiletto* spent her entire navy career of 24 years as an experimental vehicle. Five of Herreshoff's six steel-hulled torpedo boats (the *Cushing, Dupont, Talbot, Gwin,* and *Morris*) spent a total of 34 years assigned to torpedo experimentation in Newport. It is appropriate that the Bristol, Rhode Island torpedo boats (which revolutionized the design of small naval vessels and played an important role in the Spanish-American War) closed out their service careers in their home waters of Narragansett Bay, again involved in revolutionary advances in naval warfare.

Seven
The War with Spain

On April 19, 1898, Congress passed a series of resolutions that ended friendly relations between the United States and Spain. Although the Herreshoffs were no longer taking orders for boats from the navy or were involved in their construction, Herreshoff boats would be found in the coming conflict.

The Cause of the Conflict

Congressional resolutions spoke of the detestable conditions with which the citizens of Cuba had lived under Spanish rule. Of special concern was the destruction of the U.S. battleship *Maine* and the deaths of 266 crew members while the ship was on a friendly visit to Havana. It is now clear that the ship exploded because of spontaneous combustion in one of its magazines, not because of a Spanish or Cuban mine. The resulting pro-rebel sentiment, inflamed by a biased U.S. press (led by the anti-Spanish sensationalism of the Hearst and Pulitzer newspapers), caused an American outcry for revenge, making war almost inevitable.

Congress declared that the citizens of Cuba had the right to self-government and that the duty of the United States was clear: to demand the government of Spain to relinquish its authority and to withdraw its land and naval forces in the area. At the time of the congressional resolutions, Cuban nationals had been struggling against their Spanish masters for three years—since February 1895, when the revolutionaries began hostilities designed to cast out the foreign rulers.

Pres. William McKinley, in a letter to Congress dated April 1, 1898, lit the flame that Congress fanned into the fire of war. McKinley's lofty rhetoric of the ideals of a free Cuban people governing themselves overshadowed the few words that were doubtless the real reason for America's preparations for war. "Our trade has suffered," the President said, "the capital invested by our citizens in Cuba has been largely lost, and the temper and forbearance of our people have been so seriously tried as to beget a perilous unrest among our own citizens."

The actual war lasted only four months, from mid-April to mid-August 1898. The navy scored an unparalleled success by destroying the Spanish Fleet in Manila Bay in the Philippines and at Santiago Harbor on Cuba's northern coast. These almost bloodless victories satisfied Americans' desires that did so much to bring about the war.

War Becomes a Certainty

The resolutions put into effect by Congress on April 19, 1898, were signed by President McKinley, effectively ratifying their provisions. That same day, the document was forwarded to the Spanish minister in Washington, Polo y Bernabé, who demanded and received his

The Foote, Ericsson, Morris, Cushing, *and* Porter *(or* Dupont*) at the Norfolk Navy Yard,* c. *early 1900s. (Period postcard.)*

Rear Admiral Sampson and his fleet officers at Caracas, April 1899. From left to right are the following: (front row, sitting) the captain of the Indiana*; F.B. Lomis, minister to Venezuela; Admiral Sampson; Captain Chadwick of the* New York*; (back row, standing) W.W. Russell, secretary of legation; Ensign Bennett; Commander Mead of the* Marblehead*; Commander Dayton of the* Detroit*; Medical Inspector Gravitt; Lieutenant Stanton. (From* Uncle Sam's Navy.*)*

A grease-coated Whitehead torpedo is eased into the Talbot's *aft tube. (Period postcard.)*

passport and departed for Canada, posthaste. On April 21, the Spanish government gave U.S. Minister Woodford his passport, an act that thereby severed diplomatic relations between the governments of Spain and the United States.

The first move on the part of the American forces was to blockade Havana and prevent Spanish ships from entering Cuban ports with supplies. The North Atlantic Squadron, including the torpedo boats *Dupont, Porter, Winslow,* and *Foote,* departed Key West, Florida, on the morning of April 22, 1898, headed for the Florida Straits. The monitors *Terror* and *Puritan,* gunboat *Helena,* cruiser *Marblehead,* dispatch boat *Dolphin,* and the torpedo boats *Cushing* and *Ericsson* remained behind for the time being.

The Ericsson. *This vessel, built to navy specifications by the Iowa Iron Works, was a modified version of the* Cushing.

THE TORPEDO BOAT WEAPON

As reported by Lt. G.E. Armstrong of the Royal Navy,[8] the world's maritime powers possessed a number of torpedo boats at the end of 1890. France had 210; England, 206; Germany, 180; Italy, 152; Russia, 143; Austria, 61; Greece, 51; Holland, 50; Denmark, 34; China, 32; Norway and Sweden, 31; Turkey, 30; Japan, 24; Spain, 15; and Brazil, 15. The United States commissioned its first torpedo boat that year—the *Cushing*, a Herreshoff-built craft. Armstrong wrote:

> The United States still stolidly refused to take a lesson from the old world and for reasons best known to herself, refrained from building anything more than one experimental second-class boat. It is true she had not then adapted the Whitehead self-propelled torpedo; still the Howell torpedo, with certain restrictions, was adaptable for boat work. . . . In any case, it is very curious that the Power which has had more practical experience of torpedoes in actual warfare than any other, should be the least enterprising regarding them today.

As the records show, it was originally intended that a torpedo boat would not go very far from its base of operations to deliver an attack. It would either confine its service to local harbor defense or keep within the fleet area to which it was attached. It could remain afloat or be carried on the deck of a battleship or cruiser, to be lowered for service when

The Winslow, *the boat on which Ens. Worth Bagley was killed (page 93), is shown in a period stereo view card.*

The Stringham. *This 225-foot-long vessel had a 340-ton displacement and a speed of 30 miles per hour.*

at anchor in distant waters. The early torpedo boat was a small and rather fragile craft, since it was intended to carry on its work stealthily and not make general engagements. Its launching tubes and torpedoes were offensive weapons, and one or two light guns its only defensive armament.

While the United States had developed the torpedo into a primary weapon during the post–Civil War era to an extent unapproached by foreign nations, the navy failed to develop and build an adequate delivery system—the small swift torpedo boat. The Americans had not a single craft that could cope with six Spanish destroyers. When U.S. naval authorities tried to buy some equitable models in Europe, they were met with no success whatever.

America's torpedo boats were just off the drawing board, and quickly entering the fleet just in time to see action in the impending war with Spain. At the same time, the weekly journal *Scientific American* reported:

> The United States Navy does not possess a formidable flotilla of torpedo boats, but those in commission are fine specimens of their class, an with frequent additions of new boats—about twenty are building at various yards—we shall soon pass Spain, which is fairly strong in this branch. The American torpedo boats range from little fellows, like the *Stiletto,* of 31 tons displacement and 359 horsepower, to redoubtable craft like the *Stringham,* which will be of 340 tons displacement and 7,200 horsepower. Some of them will have three torpedo tubes and others but two. The flotilla in commission consists of these boats: *Cushing,* 105 tons displacement and 1,720 horsepower; *Ericsson,* 120 and 1,800; *Foote,* 142 and 2,000; *Winslow,* 142 and

> 2,000; *Gwin,* 46 1/2 and 850; *Talbot,* 46 1/2 and 850; *Porter* and *Dupont,* and the *Somers* and *Manley,* lately purchased abroad. At the time of writing, twelve torpedo boats were in process of construction in various parts of the United States.
>
> It was conceded that the United States Navy would have a remarkable torpedo boat catcher [destroyer] when the *Bailey* was completed. The *Bailey* is one of three destroyers for which Congress made appropriations. Her builder, Charles L. Seabury & Co., has promised a boat capable of a speed of 33 knots an hour.

The fleet that Spain mustered to the Caribbean in anticipation of the approaching war with the United States included no less than six torpedo boat destroyers and seven torpedo boats. The U.S. Navy did not have even one of the former and was only then receiving the first of its pod of torpedo boats just completing trials.

The Spanish torpedo boat *Ariete* was built by Thornycroft & Company, Chiswick, England, in 1889. The *Ariete*'s armament included two torpedo tubes and a battery of four 3-pound, quick-firing guns. She was 147 feet long and 14 feet abeam, and her draft was little more than 4 feet. She displaced 97 tons. Her twin screws were driven by 1,600-horsepower engines, and it was said that her best speed was 26 knots.

In 1896, Thornycroft & Company also built the torpedo boat *Fame* for the Spanish government. *Fame* had a length of 210 feet, with a depth of 31 feet 6 inches. She was 21 feet abeam and drew 5 feet 8 inches of water. She had a displacement of only 300 tons, so her 5,400-horsepower engines drove her through the water in excess of 30 knots. The *Fame,* armed with two torpedo tubes capable of launching 18-inch Whitehead torpedoes, carried one 12-pound and five 6-pound rapid-firing guns.

Spain's six torpedo boat destroyers were all Clyde-built during the years 1896–1897. These included the *Furor,* the *Terror,* the *Audaz,* the *Osado,* the *Pluton,* and the *Proserpina.*

The *Cushing* and the *Porter*

Of the several torpedo boats under construction, the Herreshoff models were the first launched and the first American-built seen by the anxious naval command. The press was no less eager to report on the beauty, speed, and stealthy efficiency of the new swift fighting machines that were to deliver the deadly submarine-torpedo weapon. In 1898, the Honorable James Rankin Young detailed some of the *Cushing* and *Porter*'s specifications in his book *War with Spain.*

> The *Cushing* was built by the Herreshoffs, as the first sea-going torpedo boat of the new United States Navy. Her specifications at the time were impressive: length, 137.5 feet; extreme breadth, 15.05; depth of hold, 9.21; draught, 4.50; displacement, 2,240 tons. Her deck and bottom plating varies from 5/64 to 1/4 inch. Double frames were placed at all water tight bulkheads, of which there were ten. The conningtowers [*sic*] were of 1/4-inch steel plate. By means of electric connections, the torpedoes could be launched from the three tubes by the *Cushing*'s commander in the conning tower. With two separate quadruple expansion engines, a speed of 23 knots could be obtained. Bunker capacity was 37 tons, and the *Cushing* had a radius of action of 3,000

"With our fleet at key west, torpedo boat 'Cushing' carrying dispatches to the flag-ship." (Drawing by Carlton T. Chapman for Harper's Weekly.*)*

> miles at ten knots an hour. Three rapid-fire six-pounder Hotchkiss breech-loading rifles and two or more Gatlings constituted the armament.
>
> The *Porter,* another type of torpedo boat—and a much faster one—maintained an average speed of 28.74 knots per hour on her trial trip for a distance of sixty miles. Convert that into statute miles, and the result is 33.1 miles [per hour]. The *Porter* went through the water with scarcely any fuss, and in war therefore, had first-call for night attacks. The *Porter* was 175 feet long and carried three torpedo-launching carriages. Her plating was very thin to save weight, and she carried one-pounder rapid-firing guns.

On May 12, 1898, with scant knowledge of where his enemy might be cruising, Adm. William T. Sampson brought his Gulf Fleet ships into position off San Juan, Puerto Rico. The seasoned mariner was spoiling for a naval engagement with the Spanish ships, but he found no trace of Admiral Cervera's fleet. Sampson could have taken Cadiz, which lay open to his guns and easy pray for a land attack, but he chose instead to keep his battle flags furled, send the torpedo boat *Porter* to Cape Haitian for dispatches, and resume his search for the elusive Spaniard.

The *Porter,* serving in a number of capacities other than as a weapons platform, returned to Sampson with important messages, and Sampson on the *New York* knew his adversary was still in coastal waters, even though the Spaniard was presumed to be low on food and fuel. Meanwhile, Sampson kept in touch with Washington via cable stations and runs by the smaller torpedo boats *Foote* and *Talbot* to Key West off the U.S. mainland.

The U.S. fleet began cruising the waters off Cuba. When Commodore Schley reported on May 29, 1898, that he had discovered Cervera's whole fleet at anchor in the port of Santiago, Adm. William T. Sampson knew his search was over. He moved his flagship, the armored cruiser *New York,* and his fleet toward Santiago, where he saw Schley at the entrance to the harbor, his ships effectively positioned to bottle up the Spanish naval forces. The blockade and the effective end of the war had begun.[9]

The torpedo boat Foote *patrolling her station.*

Eight
Torpedo Boat Adventures during the War

Ens. Worth Bagley

The following letter by Ens. Worth Bagley, a youth scarcely out of his teens who was executive officer aboard the *Winslow,* was written to his mother in May 1898.

Off Matanzas, Cuba
May 9, 1898

We are now lying off Matanzas in the middle of the entrance to the harbor three miles further in. A mile and a half away on one side are the Partia Gardia and Sabanilla batteries, and at the same distance on the other are the Maya and other batteries. Maranzas is a town of about 35,000 inhabitants with an antebellum commerce of some value. It lies, as I said before three miles inside the entrance at which we are lying, around a horseshoe or bend, which makes it not visible from our location. The batteries, however, are here at the entrance and made themselves very much in evidence yesterday by firing at the *Dupont,* which was lying too close under their fire. She got away quickly and in return for having to run, went up the coast two miles and leveled a Spanish blockhouse. The *Winslow* has not been fired at. All the large ships here left the blockade, the gunboats and torpedo boats remaining to hold it. No ship has so much as hove in sight of this entrance for days. So you may judge for yourself whether the blockhouse is effective.

Being, without news and no thing happening within our own little sphere, the monotony is absolutely painful. There are two other warships here, the torpedo boat *Dupont,* and the armed yacht *Hornet.* These two boats lie over at the eastern entrance, while we guard the western. Of course it is necessary to keep a very careful lookout at night on account of the Spanish gunboats in these waters. The caliber of their guns is greater than that of our three little 1-pounders, but we wish they would come out just the same, for we would use our torpedoes and sink them.

No one knows where the armored ships of our squadron have gone, but it is supposed that they have left to intercept the Spanish fleet off San Juan, should that port prove to be its destination.

The nation, as a whole, from the tenor of the papers, has realized that the navy is our defense, our real fighting body. The *Dupont* is coming this way, so I must have

> my letter ready for her and close now. I feel that I will hear from you when the next mail comes. Bless you, dear, for your goodness.
>
> Love to each one, and don't forget that I am in perfect safety.
> Devotedly, Worth.

Ironically, Bagley wrote this letter three days before his death by enemy action in the Bay of Gardenas on the north coast of Cuba.

It had been the intention of the commanding officer of the gunboat *Wilmington* to enter the harbor on the afternoon of May 11, 1898, but because of the draft of the vessel, this action was reconsidered. Among the three channels leading to the city of Gardenas, two were known to be mined, and the third had a depth of only 1.75 fathoms and was yet to be explored. Additionally, camouflaged batteries were supposed to exist along the shore. When a small Spanish gunboat was observed moored to a wharf some distance away, the *Winslow* was ordered to go in and take her out.

With her torpedoes set for surface runs, and the charges set to explode at short range, the little *Winslow,* with Bagley, steamed onto the harbor on her mission. When she had reached a distance of 1,500 yards from the Spanish gunboat, the first shots of the encounter rained down around the *Winslow* from the shore batteries calculating their range.

Alas, it turned out that Bagley was not "in perfect safety." His story became a subject in Josephus Daniels's *The First Fallen Hero.* On April 29, 1898, a *New York Herald* correspondent had interviewed Bagley aboard the *Winslow,* where the ensign confided to the reporter his edginess about the so-called torpedo fleet. He mentioned fellow sailors, such as "poor Breckenridge," his classmate aboard the *Cushing,* who was swept overboard between Key West and Havana and drowned. Breckenridge's successor on the *Cushing,* Baldwin, was knocked down a hatchway and suffered broken ribs. Another, Executive Officer Bostwick of the *Ericsson,* was knocked overboard during a collision with a schooner and all but drowned. Yet another *Cushing* executive officer, Boyd, also met with an accident, and Bagley wondered to the newspaper correspondent about his chances.

> There they are, the four "B's"—Breckinridge, Bostwick, Baldwin and Boyd. I am the fifth and last—Bagley. I have never been superstitious, but for a week I have had mysterious intuitions that I am not to escape. I will make the list complete—of that I am certain. I only hope that my trouble will not be serious to take me out of the fight.[10]

'The Rescue of the *Winslow*'

The following account by Lt. Ernest E. Mead, navigating officer aboard the *Hudson,* tells the story of the *Winslow.*[11]

> The engagement between the American vessels and Spanish gunboats off Cardenas, May 11, 1898, in no way quickened or retarded the natural outcome of hostilities; but to us it was the most sanguine naval action of the war, and it showed one phase of that

Ens. Worth Bagley of the Winslow. *Ensign Bagley was the first U.S. Navy officer killed by enemy action in the Spanish-American War. (From* The First Fallen Hero.*)*

The battle of Cardenas. The gunboat Wilmington, *the revenue cutter* Hudson, *and the torpedo boat* Winslow *are shown under fire.*

reckless daring and cool effrontery displayed by American soldiers and sailors.

Early on the morning of May 11, the *Machias* and *Hudson,* cruising off the keys, made out a strange smoke, to which they gave chase. The stranger was the gunboat *Wilmington.* The *Machias* hoisted the signal, "Follow the motions of this vessel," led the way in, by the outer anchorage, to an anchorage close up to Diana Key. Here, shortly before nine o'clock in the morning, the *Machias* and *Wilmington* anchored. The *Hudson* was sent to explore a partly obstructed passage to the eastward of Diana Key. For over an hour the *Hudson* quartered the round, sounding out a tortuous and almost impracticable channel.

On her return to the squadron, which had meanwhile been augmented by the torpedo boat *Winslow,* the *Hudson* was directed to accompany the *Winslow* and take soundings in Surjidero Pass, while the *Wilmington* shifted her anchorage somewhat to the eastward to cover operations.

Shortly before noon the American squadron, consisting of the *Wilmington, Winslow,* and *Hudson,* steamed into Cardenas Bay in search of the Spanish gunboats.

Preceded by the smaller vessels, the *Wilmington* picked her way slowly through the channel into the bay. Here she took the lead, and, with the *Hudson* on her starboard and the *Winslow* on her port quarter, well clear of her guns, proceeded toward Cardenas.

When about half-way across the bay, the *Hudson* was ordered to skirt the then invisible [shrouded in fog] western shore, and attack and destroy, capture or drive in, any gunboats which might be hidden close under the land.

The *Hudson* soon passed the buoys of the main ship-channel; and then, seeing nothing of the expected gunboats, we turned and followed the general curve of the shore toward the town. The officers searched with their glasses every little bay and creek in hopes of seeing a concealed gunboat. This profitless search was soon finished, and glasses and vessel were turned toward Cardenas, which the *Wilmington,* followed closely by the *Winslow,* was rapidly nearing.

More than a mile off the western end of the town, where the water was deep enough, were anchored two square-rigged vessels, showing no colors, and without a soul on board. Toward these the *Wilmington* was heading. Moving so slowly as to make scarcely a ripple, she steamed down close to them, and changing her course to the eastward, ranged along parallel to the shore, about two miles distant from it. As there was still no sign of resistance, the *Winslow* closed in with the intention of drawing the Spanish gunboats from their hiding-places and inducing them to give battle in the open. Bravely she glided in, feeling her way as the water rapidly shoaled, until little more than half a mile from the wharves.

Then, from behind the corner of one of the piers, came a flash, followed by a faint puff of vapor, and a shell screamed past her. Before the *Winslow* could turn, from three or four other places came the smokeless flash, and again, and with greater precision, the destructive projectiles.

Before the report of the first gun had reached us, the *Wilmington* belched forth a sheet of flame. The clouds of smoke rising from it proclaimed that the fight had begun.

Following at full speed, as closely as possible in the wake of the other vessels, the *Hudson,* about ten minutes after the *Wilmington* opened fire, passed between the two sailing-vessels anchored off the western end of the town, and being then in range, opened fire with her bow gun. The dense smoke around the flag-ship made it impossible to read the signals, so the *Hudson* hauled up more to the eastward, thus bringing her after-gun also to bear, and ran down to within hailing distance of the *Wilmington.* Receiving orders to go in closer, we rounded the bow of the *Wilmington,* and moving to about three thousand yards of the shore, turned to the westward keeping up a constant fire on the largest wharf.

The smoke from our guns was so thick that the shore was often hidden, but a few hundred yards inshore, and somewhat to the east, an occasional glimpse was caught of the gallant little *Winslow* banging away with her 1-pounders.

Except for the flashes on shore, those on the *Hudson* would not have known there was an enemy. It was well indeed for the Spanish gunboats that they had the friendly shelter of the solid wharves behind which they were concealed, for in the open they could not have lived five minutes in the face of the *Wilmington*'s terrific fire. The sharp cracking explosion of the 6-pounders put an edge to the roar of the heavier guns, sounding often as one report. Each concussion of our little guns shook the *Hudson* from stem to stern, while to those serving them it was like a box on the ears.

From the beginning of the engagement the sole efforts of the Spanish gunners had been to disable the torpedo boat. One of the first shots fired struck her and partly lamed her. Fairly deluged with shot and shell, struck in a dozen places, she still fought on, and it was not until her steering-gear was injured and she became nearly unmanageable that her commander thought of withdrawing.

As we turned for the second time to the eastward, the *Winslow* came darting out of the smoke clouds directly toward us. A slight shifting of the *Hudson*'s helm allowed us to pass close to her. Hailing us, the commanding office of the *Winslow* told us he intended to withdraw his crippled command from the fire of the Spanish guns.

Turning again to the eastward, we moved up toward the *Wilmington,* trying to give the *Winslow* sufficient room in which to turn and work out of the enemy's fire. As we turned, our attention was called to the *Winslow*. Her machinery was stopped, and she was rapidly drifting toward shore. Unable to read [the quartermaster's wig-wag signal] we ran within hailing distance, and at last heard Lieutenant Bernadou shout that his vessel was totally disabled.

With the after-gun's crew ready to handle the lines, the *Hudson* was steered for the *Winslow,* close enough to throw a heaving-line to her. As we forged ahead across her bow, the heaving-line was thrown. It fell short. Reversing engines, and putting the helm to starboard, the captain of the *Hudson* tried to back his vessel down to the *Winslow;* but working directly against her helm, the *Hudson* backed around until she was bows on to the *Winslow,* and moving away from her. With every minute that passed the helpless *Winslow* neared the shore, and into a zone of more murderous fire.

Backward and forward, swerving this way and that, the *Hudson* struggled for more than twenty minutes at a task that each moment grew more hopeless. At last fortunate sheer, a quick shift of the helm, the line was thrown, caught, the hawser was bent on, and the two little craft started to draw away from their most dangerous position.

As we were approaching the *Winslow* on our second attempt to close with her the tragic event which has given this engagement its sad prominence occurred. The officers and crew of the *Winslow* were gathered along her rail waiting to grasp the expected heaving-line. Grouped around the starboard gun were an officer [Ens. Worth Bagley] and four men. They stood there, the men, expectant, every nerve taut, waiting to grasp the elusive line, which was their only chance to escape almost certain destruction—the officer, self-contained, smiling, a perfect antidote for nervousness in his calm bearing. the next instant they were gone. A flash, barely visible in the glare of the sun, a report, unnoticed in the noise of battle, a faint puff of vapor, and as it cleared away we realized that five of our comrades in danger had been wounded, killed, destroyed by an enemy's projectile.

One poor fellow, falling on the curve of the deck, was slipping overboard, when he made a last despairing grasp at a stanchion and held on, calling plaintively for help. A shriek of horror rose from both crews as his shipmates sprang to his assistance. He never knew of their ready answer to his call. He was dead when they tenderly drew his body back on deck. One cry, a few muttered curses and the crews hurried to their stations; some to their guns to work them as they had never been worked before, the others to the seemingly hopeless task of saving both vessels.

At last the line was made fast, and we started out toward the *Wilmington,* which had all this time been keeping up that terrific fire which eventually silenced the Spanish guns, and all but destroyed the water-front of the town. As we drew near her, feeling

The battle of Cardenas, with the Winslow *under fire. In this view, the revenue cutter* Hudson *and the gunboat Wilmington return fire on the Winslow. (Painting by William Ritschel.)*

that we were now reasonably safe, she ceased firing, and turning, led the way toward the outer bay.

As we drew away from the town a small tongue of flame stole up one corner of the largest warehouse. It spread rapidly, and before we were out of sight the whole structure was in flames. weeks afterward we learned from deserters from the town that fifteen minutes more of our fire would have caused the surrender of the town, gunboats, and all the shipping.

Later that night the *Hudson* started for Key West with the sad tidings, bearing as her witness the dead and wounded—the wounded to the loving care of their countrymen, the dead to a resting-place in their own country.

SERVICE ABOARD THE *PORTER*

The following excerpt is from *Torpedo-boat Service,* by Lt. John C. Fremont of the U.S. Navy, commanding the *Porter*. It was published in November 1898 in *Harper's New Monthly Magazine.*

Torpedo-boats are the race-horses of the steamer world, built for short dashes at high speed. Yet during the earlier part of the Spanish war circumstances forced the use of our torpedo-boats for long-continued strains in weather that proved trying to the much larger vessels that were with them. The discomforts and the trials borne by their crews during this period will never be known, nor could they be appreciated by

"The 'Porter' engaging the batteries off San Juan." (From Harper's New Monthly Magazine, *November 1898.)*

any one but those who were in the service.

The *Porter* is a vessel about 175 feet long and 17.5 feet wide—ten times her own beam in length. She draws but little water—her hull less than five feet. Her rudder and propellers project below the hull so as to get the fullest and most unobstructed effect on the water. Her hull is constructed in the strongest and lightest manner consistent with the power it has to contain. The thickness of the hull plating—except in certain stringers meant to take strains—is only one-tenth of an inch, and the framing and construction generally are in proportion to this. But even after what the *Porter* has been through, her hull is as good as the day it was built, not a leak having developed nor anything giving away. Into this frail craft are put three boilers and two main engines, developing the tremendous energy of 4000 horse-power, and capable of driving the boat over thirty knots, or with the speed of a railroad train. Many other engines, pumps, evaporators, etc., are crowded into the vessel, until five-sevenths of the ship are taken up with machinery and coal; the other two-sevenths—the extreme ends—are left, and into these is put the boat's crew—officers forward, men aft. But even into these spaces are introduced engines—anchor engines, steering engines; and steam-pipes for various purposes lead through all, rendering them unbearably hot in a tropical climate. Torpedo-boats are a compact mass of machinery, not meant to keep the sea and to live in, but to be used for short runs out from a base, to which they can return at any time and find rest for the crew and repair facilities for their machinery. The exigencies of the earlier part of this war required them to be used otherwise, and that the boats and their crews have so creditably sustained the unusual test is a matter for congratulation to their builders and to the service.

April 22 found the torpedo-boats tuned up to the highest pitch and anxious for a chance to try themselves, and it was with great hopes and unlimited enthusiasm that we started across to Havana that memorable morning.

It was rough—rough even for the Gulf Stream—and that day and night showed us that the life on board the *Porter* was going to be a struggle with nature, a test of physical endurance. The *Porter*'s motion is such a sharp sea as nearly all the time runs off the coast of Cuba is, to say the least, uncomfortable. The roll is from 30 to 45 degrees each way, and twenty-five times a minute, with occasionally an extra roll thrown in, which goes beyond the registering limit of the indicators, and makes you wonder why she takes the trouble to come back, it seems so much easier just to go on all the way round.

To rest and sleep in such conditions is very difficult, and is only possible when physical exhaustion overcomes every other feeling; and then the sleep is so broken that it ill fits one to renew the exacting duties of handling the delicate mechanisms of the boats, or exercise the cool judgment and instant decision demanded by the service.

In addition to this, the heat below was such that no one went there except on duty. The life was on deck: those on duty at their posts were on their feet; the remainder, if not struggling with their very simple meals, were trying to get some sleep, stretched out and wedged in between torpedo-tubes and rail or in some place that prevented their sliding round.

Hopes that our chance had come [for a fight] were high on the *Porter* the first day off Havana. A man-of-war was sighted under the land, and the *New York, Marblehead, Wilmington,* and *Porter* started in for her; but it turned out to be an Italian and the only guns used were those fired in salute. Immediately afterwards the *Porter*'s sorrow at the lost opportunity was partly assuaged by the capture of a schooner within range of the guns of the eastern batteries of Havana. When the crew of the schooner found they were not to be murdered at once, as they had been led to believe, they were not only reconciled to their fate, but voluntarily gave us information of more sugar-laden vessels due the next day. The roughness and tedium of that day were easily endured in the hope of more prizes on the morrow, the hopes were realized; daylight found the *Porter* steaming slowly for the flag-ship to report, with a 2300-ton schooner-load of sugar in tow.

This ended the first forty-eight hours of the war.

A Close Shave for the *Porter*

The following, from Young's *Reminiscence,* is a log entry by Ens. Irving V. Gillis, aboard the *Porter,* with Lt. John C. Fremont as captain.

> We were in action at San Juan. It seemed as if the entire shore opened fire on us at once. When it is considered that a bullet from a Mauser rifle would go clear through our hull, the effect of a shell striking us may be imagined. We immediately opened fire, however, with our one pounders, and are confident one battery was made much

> less valuable by the attentions of the *Porter*. We were signaled to retire to safer quarters, and made our way out at once. While retiring I sat on the steps to the upper structure forward. I saw a six-pounder shot coming and remarked that it looked as though it would land. The shot passed three feet above my head and fell into the water astern, scarcely clearing the after portion of the *Porter*. Another shot came from the same battery while we lay broadside toward it, and went over our heads by only a little.

THE *PORTER* AVERTS A COSTLY ERROR

The story of the torpedo boat *Porter*'s mistaking the flagship of the U.S. fleet for an enemy vessel is one of the better documented incidents of the Spanish-American War. On patrol in fog and darkness, the *Porter* had orders to challenge any strange ship and blow her out of the water if she proved to be the enemy's.

The *New York* was some distance from her blockading station and displayed no lights except for an occasional signal light. The usually reliable signal apparatus of the *New York* failed this particular night; it was the cause that nearly brought the ship to its end.

In the night, American ships recognized each other in two ways—by the position of the vessel, which was her night station and, failing that, by use of signal lights. If the stranger failed to answer the signal light properly and promptly, the ship's batteries would be manned, and the ship would close in to get the stranger's range for killing fire. An eyewitness account was recorded for history.[12]

> It was grim work in the dark, but Lieutenant Fremont, ever cheerful, went about his scout duty with the complacency of a man whose mind was easy. We cruised westward. I lay down on deck near a 1-pounder—too close. Lieutenant Fremont went below for a nap. Ensign Gillis was in charge of the *Porter* for the time. There was quiet until half-past two in the morning.
>
> Then the 1-pounder beside me woke me as thoroughly as if it had been a 13-inch gun, and I raced to the conning tower to see what had happened, and saw what seemed to the very biggest ship in the world looming up on our port bow, indistinct in the gloom, but close enough to sink us without fail a second after the order to fire.
>
> We had fired across her bow to stop her and learn if she were friend or foe. Foe it seemed she was, for our guns were trained on her, and the port torpedo was ready to leap from its tube and do for her what we expected she would do for us in a second or two.

Lieutenant Fremont stood before the conning tower. Gillis had made out the loom of the stranger when they were a quarter of a mile away and had awakened his commander. Silently the *Porter* stole upon the warship. When they were only about 200 yards away and within easy signal distance, the night fleet signal light was flashed by the torpedo boat. The record continues:

> Two white lights and one red. It burned for a second or so, and then it was turned off. There was no reply. The stranger, dark and unheeding, moved slowly westward.

"Bad Weather." (From Harper's New Monthly Magazine, *November 1898.)*

That she had not seen it was inconceivable, for there were twenty men looking out for signals on every American warship at this time, and no one could believe that they'd overlooked that well-known signal flashed clear so close at hand.

The *Porter* shot close, so close that every man on her felt that desperate work was in hand, and that now we were in it beyond recall.

Our blowers were making a loud, droning noise. The movement of both vessels through the water added to the difficulty of hearing. Fremont's voice rose so that I thought it must have rung through the strange ship. But the crew of the strange ship were rushing to their guns.

'Stop those damned blowers,' Fremont said.

'Are the guns trained on her?' he asked.

'Aye, aye, sir,' came from both 1-pounders. The torpedo, too, was ready. It had been tested for pressure but a few hours earlier. As each Jackie answered 'Aye, aye, sir,' his commander's voice rang out again. This time he was hailing. The voice was

The Porter *comes under the guns of the* New York.

very stern and menacing, and the inflection rising: 'What-ship-is-that?'

No answer, 'Fire across her bow.' Bang! went our bow gun, and the metal rattled as the men shoved another shell home, and trained the piece again.

'Show the night fleet signal,' Fremont said, and flashed again—two white lights above a red one. We were under the stranger's quarter now, close aboard. For one of us there was no escape. At that range a torpedo must destroy the big ship inevitably.

A second after our signal burned, the stranger's signal mast blazed, and there hung an answering signal, but not the right one, there burned two red ones and a white one. For a moment it flashed through Fremont's mind that the enemy might be attempting to use the American signals.

There was no time to think about it. There was a flash from the stranger's forward fighting top, and a shell whistled over us. We believed that rifles and machine guns would be riddling us a second later. The big guns could not be depressed enough to bear on us, so close were we. Fremont had been hailing at the moment, and his face had been turned away from that top from which the gun was fired.

'Did that shot come from her?' he shouted.

'Yes, sir,' said a Jackie and I in the same breath.

All these things had occupied but a few moments, passing with inconceivable rapidity. For a second, perhaps, Lieutenant Fremont stood still and silent, and his men waited for a word which would turn loose a torpedo from the *Porter,* and a hail of fire from the flagship.

'What-ship-is-that?'

'This is the *New York*!'

'Is that Captain Chadwick?'

'Yes,' answered the *New York*'s captain; 'is that the *Porter*?'

'Yes, sir'

'Why didn't you show the night-fleet signal?'

'We did, sir, twice. There was no answer the first time. The second time—just now—the *New York* displayed the wrong signal.'

In a subsequent inquiry, it turned out that Rear Admiral Sampson, aboard his flagship, had been awake and witnessed the entire incident. The Admiral vindicated the actions taken by the *Porter.*

"I saw the *Porter*'s signal displayed, and there was no answer from this vessel." Sampson said.

THE *PORTER* CAPTURES A SOUVENIR

The *Porter* did finish her tour of duty with the blockade in Cuban waters with a first-class *prise de guerre,* however, when she captured an 18-foot German Schwartzkopf torpedo. It was recovered by Ens. Irving Gillis, who dove into the water to keep the torpedo from striking the *Porter* when the ship was some 14 miles east of Santiago, on June 3, 1898.

It was night and the Spanish torpedo boat destroyer *Pluton* launched several Schwartzkopf torpedoes with their war noses toward the entrance of the harbor. Admiral Cervera, praying to Providence to guide them, expected the deadly missiles to pass up the channel, along

The heroic capture of an armed Schwartzkopf torpedo by Ens. Irving V. Gillis of the Porter. *(Drawing by F. Cressan Schell.)*

with the strong ebb tide, and run into any unlucky American ship they might encounter. Having spent their source of locomotion, the torpedoes floated helplessly in the rough water, farther out to open sea. In the contemporary *War with Spain,* James Rankin Young gives in vivid detail the youthful Ensign Gillis's story of valor:

> Captain Fremont, of the *Porter,* with his glass in hand, and Ensign Irving Gillis by his side, stepped to the gunwales of his boat from the main companionway and scanned the scene. . . . Something was about to occur in a few moments, something that would thrill the officers and men of the *Porter,* for in a very few moments Captain Fremont detected something coming toward his ship on the swell of the tide. It glistened aft and was black and porpoise-like forward.
>
> He did not need his glass to detect a Schwartzkopf torpedo floating along toward the *Porter.* It was not moving rapidly; but it seemed to come out of the gray mists of the morning as though seeking something to destroy.
>
> Ensign Gillis saw it too. In almost a single motion he had tossed his officer's coat on the deck and had slipped from his canvas shoes. With his hands on the rail he leaned forward and watched the terrible instrument coming toward the ship, rising

> and falling, and still approaching, nose on with each swell of the sea.
>
> An instant after she struck the *Porter* there would be nothing left to tell or show where the ship had gone down. Gillis clutched the rail firmly and prepared to make the jump.
>
> 'Don't do it, Gillis; she's got her war nose on!' exclaimed the Captain, reaching for his Ensign.
>
> 'I'll fix that, sir,' replied Gillis, leaping into the sea before his superior officer could restrain him. With a couple of strong strokes he reached the side of the Schwartzkopf and circled the nose with his arm. From the deck of the *Porter,* Captain Fremont gazed breathlessly at the daring boy tossing about in the water beneath him.
>
> Gillis quickly turned the nose of the weapon away from the *Porter,* screwed the firing pin up tightly, so that it could not operate, and then swam back to the side of the torpedo boat, pulling his prize at his side. Lifting his dripping hand from the water he saluted his captain and waited with his arm around the now harmless torpedo for further orders.

The $3,000 value of the captured 1,000-pound torpedo was awarded to Ensign Gillis. The eventual destination of the weapon was the Naval Torpedo Station at Newport, where it was dismantled and its secrets evaluated. Today, that Schwartzkopf torpedo is occasionally exhibited at the Naval War College Museum, at Newport's Naval Education and Training Center.

At the end of the war, other Schwartzkopf torpedoes were captured and were also taken to Newport. At one time, the Newport torpedo station had so many of the captured German torpedoes that they were used as lamp posts at the navy's ferryboat landing!

Ens. Irving V. Gillis attempting to unscrew the war nose on the Spanish Schwartzkopf torpedo. (From Harper's New Monthly Magazine, *November 1898.)*

Throwing a line to the Winslow. *(From* Harper's New Monthly Magazine, *November 1898.)*

Summary

While rarely used for the purposes that the Herreshoffs designed it, the torpedo boat's presence in the Spanish-American War was to have a significant effect on future naval tactics and stratagems. As Willis J. Abbot pointed out in *Blue Jackets of 1898,* the torpedo boats in service during the war with Spain were used "for every purpose except that for which they were designed." Abbot continues:

> They served as messengers and as blockaders; they bombarded fortifications, as in the case of the *Winslow* at Cardenas, and the *Porter* at San Juan; they helped in cable-cutting, and they examined rivers and harbors under the enemy's fire.

However, the miniature torpedo boat had the potential to wreak devastation on the vastly larger and often lumbering major vessels of a naval flotilla. They could often be well-nigh invisible, with their low-in-the-water profile and dark camouflage paint. Just the psychological presence of the swift "hornets of the sea" kept the crews of the large warships under great stress. As another contemporary, John R. Spears, wrote in *Our Navy in the War with Spain* (1898), "the men . . . came to see torpedo-boat ghosts—the men who fired at a hole in the rocks, and at a trade-wind swell, and at a rail-road train ashore, each time thinking they saw a torpedo-boat—these men speak of the 'night demons of the sea' with respect."

One of the near mishaps of the war occurred when that unidentified man-of-war loomed before the *Porter*, captained by John C. Fremont, during the blockade at Santiago. Had Fremont acted on impulse rather than spending the time to think things through and

The deck of the Winslow. *(From* Harper's New Monthly Magazine, *November 1898.)*

ultimately determine the "intruder" to be friendly, the 500-man *New York*, flagship of Rear Admiral Sampson's fleet might easily have been done in by the small torpedo boat and its crew of fewer than three dozen men.

Thus, the torpedo boats of Bristol proved versatile in numerous roles, and their presence in the conflict gave the navy more than sufficient reason to reconsider the entire fleet composition, including its own self-protection as well as strengthening its overall effectiveness. While not placing any more orders directly with Herreshoff Manufacturing Company, Herreshoff boats were still to find their way into U.S. naval service through intermediary purchase routes.

In 1938, the boatyard came under the control of the prominent Rhode Island industrialist Rudolf F. Haffenreffer, as president, and his son Carl W. Haffenreffer, as vice president and general manager. R.F. Haffenreffer III was treasurer, and F.W. Haffenreffer was assistant general manager. During the World War II years, the yard built 100 wooden-hulled military vessels (motor torpedo boats, or PTs, as well as aircraft rescue boats, minesweepers, and coastal transports), including eight 71-foot (English) Vosper PT boats. Twenty were U.S. Navy PT boats that were delivered to the navy of the USSR. Up to that time, the Herreshoff Manufacturing Company had found another niche in maritime construction as designers and builders of pleasure yachts, continuing the long tradition begun in 1893 with the *Vigilant* and other America's Cup defenders.

The torpedo boat Winslow. *"This little vessel, dangerous for her minuteness, as her efficiency depends largely upon her ability to escape detection, was brought into special prominence on May 12 by a terrible tragedy enacted upon her decks. In company of the gunboat 'Wilmington' and armed revenue cutter 'Hudson,' the 'Winslow' entered Cardenas Bay, Cuba, to attack the defenses of Cardenas, and three small Spanish gunboats that had taken refuge in the harbor. The 'Winslow,' being of light draught, advanced within 800 yards of the forts and was fired upon with disastrous effect, being struck no less than eighteen times. When their boat became helpless from her hurts, the crew signaled the 'Hudson' for help, which promptly responded, but while a tow-line was being made fast a shell from the enemy burst in the face of the group of the 'Winslow's' crew on deck, killing three and wounding as many more, among the former being Ensign Worth Bagley, twenty-five years of age, who had recently entered active service. Lieutenant John B. Bernadou, in command, was badly wounded in the leg, and soon after two other men fell under the murderous fire of the Spaniards. For more than an hour the frail little craft was at the enemy's batteries, but every survivor was a hero, and by the 'Hudson's' aid, and an exhibition of the extraordinary courage, she was towed out of range, and brought to Key West, where the bodies were prepared for burial, and the vessel was placed in repair. Bagley was the first sacrifice of the war on the American side. The 'Winslow' is 160 feet 4 inches in length, 16 feet in breadth and of 5 feet mean draught. She is of 2000 horse power, has a speed of 24 1/2 knots, cost $97,000, and has an armament of three 1-pound rapid-fire guns and three 18-inch Whitehead torpedoes." (From* Harper's New Monthly Magazine, *November 1898.)*

Nine
The *Cushing* in Newport

The subject of the following Newport torpedo station correspondence (dated July 21, 1888, and designated No. 893) deals with the qualities of a Swedish-built torpedo boat.

[To] The Chief of the Bureau of Ordnance,
Navy Department,
Washington, D.C.

Sir:
In obedience to the Bureau's order contained in the second endorsement on No. 1546. I have the honor to report that the papers and model submitted by Commodore Th. Areidsson of the Bergsund Engineering and Shipbuilding Co. of Stockholm, Sweden have been considered at the Torpedo Station and to submit the following remarks.

Commodore Arvidsson makes a radical departure in design from that generally accepted for sea going torpedo boats, with a view to obtaining better protection for the vital parts. This aim has been re[a]lized though, to a certain extent, at the sacrifice of other desirable qualities. The draught of water is greater than in the ordinary type, but not greater than what may be regarded as permissible. It would seem that greater engine power must be needed to drive this boat than on of the ordinary shape - but this fact can only be established by actual trial.

The stability of the proposed boat according to the Commodore's calculations appears ample. Her behavior at sea can be determined by experiments. The shape of her underwater body ought to tend to check uneasiness induced by her great beam and the lowness of her weight but, as the speed is guaranteed, this omission may not be important.

The price for which it is proposed to deliver a boat of this design, guaranteed as to speed and built, is extremely low.

What disposition is to be made of the model and papers?

Respectfully,
Your obedient servant
C.F. Goodrich, Commander, USN

Torpedo boats at dock in Newport Harbor at Goat Island. From left to right are the Winslow, Stiletto, Morris, *and* Porter. *The Fall River–New York overnight steamer* Pilgrim *is in the far left background. (NTS photograph.)*

Acceptance of the *Cushing*

Navy Department,
Washington,
April 12, 1890.

Sir:

I have to inform you that the Herreshoff Manufacturing Company, of Bristol, Rhode Island, contractors for the construction of Torpedo Boat No. 1, have been directed to deliver said vessel at the Torpedo Station, Newport, R.I., at as early a date as may be practicable. In order, therefore, that the Department may be fully informed as to the condition in which the vessel is when delivered at said Station, and as to whether the contractors have supplied all the articles to be furnished by them under their contract, you will please direct the officer superintending the construction of said vessel to proceed in her to said station when she is delivered there by the contractors, and after an examination of the vessel there, to report, in duplicate, to the officer in charge of the station whether or not the vessel is in the condition required by the contract and to furnish the officer in charge of the station with a certificate, in duplicate, stating whether or not all articles to be furnished by the contractors are on board her, together with a list, also in duplicate, showing specifically what articles are on board the vessel and what, if any, of the articles required are not on board her.

You will also instruct the officer in charge of said station to be prepared to receive the vessel on her arrival at the station, on her delivery to receive a receipt for her to the contractors, and upon the receipt of the reports and lists from the Inspectors, to forward the originals thereof to the Department, retaining the duplicates in his office.

Very respectfully,
F.M. RAMSAY
Acting Secretary of the Navy

Bureau of Ordnance,
Navy Department
Washington City, April 14, 1890
Subject: Acceptance of *Cushing*
In reply refer to No. 1331
[To] Comdr. Theo. F. Jewell, U.S.N.
Inspector of Ordnance In Charge,
Naval Torpedo Station and War College,
Newport, R.I.

Sir:
The Bureau forwards, for compliance therewith, a copy of a letter from the Honorable Secretary of the Navy, directing the acceptance of the *Cushing,* etc., etc.

You will please proceed with the local member of the Board, recently ordered to witness the trials of this vessel, that is to say, in company with Lieut. T.C. McLean, U.S.N., to Bristol, R.I. in the *Stiletto,* and return to the Naval Torpedo Station and

The Cushing *steaming past Goat Island. The* Cushing*'s sleek uncluttered lines can be admired in this full starboard view. She was modeled after the Herreshoff Manufacturing Company's fast steam yachts. Buildings of the Naval Torpedo Station at Newport are visible in the background.*

War College in the *Cushing*, testing her distilling apparatus, which you are aware is still on trial. If, upon your arrival at Newport, the distilling apparatus works to your satisfaction, and the vessel, including this apparatus, is in all respects as per contract, you will, as directed by the letter of the Honorable Secretary of the Navy, receive the *Cushing* at the Torpedo Station and deliver to the Contractors or their agents the enclosed bills in their favor. In case these conditions are not fulfilled, you will report the circumstances, retaining the bills until further instructions.

Lieut. C. McR. Winslow, U.S.N., and others will be ordered to-day to command her after which she will be directed to proceed to the Navy Yard, Washington, D.C.

I am, Sir, Your obedt. Servt.
W.M. Folger
Chief of Bureau.

Naval Torpedo Station and War College,
Newport, R.I
April 17, 1890
[To] Chief of the Bureau of Ordnance,
Navy Department,
Washington, D.C.

In obedience to the Bureau's instructions of April 14, 1890 (No. 1331) I proceeded to Bristol in the *Stiletto* yesterday, the 16th inst., accompanied by Lieut. T.C. McLean and returned to the Torpedo Station in the *Cushing*. Tests were made of the distilling apparatus as directed, while lying at the wharf at Bristol and while underway in the bay. The apparatus failed entirely to give fresh water, but as it seemed from the extreme saltiness of the water delivered by it that there might be some leakage through the valves, further trial was postponed until today, at the suggestion of the contractors.

Upon the arrival of the boat at the Station today, the distiller was in operation both cylinders of the distiller being used as evaporators, the resulting steam being delivered in the main condensers. There is no possible means, when the distiller is used in this manner, of determining whether the water produced is salt or fresh.

The after cylinder was then used as the evaporator, the forward one as the condenser, and during some twenty minutes the apparatus delivered cool water having a slight taste of oily water, due to the newness of some of the connections, at the rate of 12 1/2 gallons per hour or 300 gallons per day.

The arrangement of the connections was then changed so that the forward cylinder became the evaporator and the after one the condenser. The resulting water was salt. The gauge glass showed considerable foaming in the evaporator. The contractors claim that this does not necessarily indicate that salt water was being carried over with the steam, since the steam exit is some distance above the upper end of the water gauge.

The cylinders were then reversed again, the after one being made the evaporator, the forward on the condenser. The water was at first salt, but afterwards when the water level was carried some distance above the coil through which the heating steam was led and a slight pressure maintained in the evaporating cylinder, good water, free from salt, was obtained.

As the operation of the distilling apparatus was not satisfactory, I declined to receive the *Cushing* and have retained the contractor's vouchers to await your further instructions.

When it works properly the distiller certainly gives a copious supply of good water, but it requires very close attention and the contractors admit that it often fails to work in the most unaccountable way. I consider it a serious defect that it is impossible to tell whether the water is salt or not when both cylinders are used as evaporators, the resulting steam being condensed in the main condenser. It might readily occur that the boilers were thus being fed with salt water and no one be the wiser.

The design of the distiller seems to be a good one, and were it not for the unsuccessful efforts of the contractors to make it work reliably at all times, I should say that more experience might overcome the difficulties at present met with. But their experience is not encouraging.

Very respectfully,
Your obedient servant,
Theo. F. Jewell, Commander, U.S.N.

[To] The Herreshoff Manufacturing Co.,
Bristol, R.I.
April 19th 1890

Gentlemen:
The Department is in receipt of your telegram of the 17th instant, in which, after referring to the failure of the distilling apparatus of Torpedo Boat No. 1, the "Cushing", to meet the requirements of the contract on the recent test of the same while the vessel was lying at the wharf at Bristol, and while under way in the bay, en route to the Torpedo Station for delivery, you state that you propose to take the distilling apparatus out of the vessel, perfect it without delay and put in a satisfactory condition for inspection by officers appointed for that purpose, and request that the Department accept the vessel now, subject to a special reservation of $1000. to be held until the distilling apparatus shall be completed, tested and accepted as required by the contract, and issue instructions to the officer in charge of the Torpedo Station to receive the vessel.

It appearing from the report of Commander Jewell, dated the 17th instant, that the failure of the distilling apparatus of the "Cushing" constitutes a serious defect in the machinery of the vessel, the Departments is of the opinion that, in addition to the special reservation of $1000. to be held on account thereof as provided in the Department's letter to you of the 12th instant, the "special reserve" of $5000., provided for in the 11th clause of the contract, should be held subject not only to the conditions stated in that clause, but subject also to the completion, testing and acceptance of the distilling apparatus. If the Herreshoff Manufacturing Company shall assent to the withholding of the two reservations, amounting to $6000., under the conditions above stated, and in the vessel, or to substitute therefor one meeting all the requirements of the contract and specifications, such work to be done at the Company's yard, where the vessel will be sent and remain while the work is being done, in charge of an officer of the Navy, the Company is requested to signify such assent formally, in writing, the Department, and on the receipt thereof the Department will issue instructions by telegram for the acceptance of the vessel accordingly.

Very respectfully,
B.F. Tracy
Secretary of the Navy.

The following letter from the Herreshoff Manufacturing Company to the secretary of the U.S. Navy is dated April 20, 1890:

Sir:

Referring to the Department's communication dated April 19th, regarding the distilling apparatus of Torpedo Boat No. 1., "Cushing."

We hereby assent to the withholding of the two reservations amounting to $6,000.00, under the conditions stated in the above mentioned communication,

This view of the Cushing *inaccurately shows a torpedo tube projecting from the hull aft of her bow. The inset in the lower left shows the Herreshoff Manufacturing Company yard at Bristol, Rhode Island. In the upper right is a view of the* Cushing*'s stern.*

The Cushing*'s clear decks. This view shows the distinctive curve of the* Cushing*'s bow, unencumbered by protruding torpedo tubes. The protected deadlights are visible in the* Cushing*'s bulwarks—a feature carried over from the* Stiletto *and the Herreshoffs' other steam yachts.*

and will proceed, without delay, to perfect the distilling apparatus made for the vessel, or to substitute therefor one meeting all the requirements of the contract and specifications, such work to be done at our Yard, where the vessel is to be sent and remain while the work is being done.

In conformity with the above agreement, the "Cushing" is ready for immediate delivery.

Very respectfully,
Herreshoff Mfg. Co.
John B. Herreshoff, Treas.

Office of Inspector of Sea-going Torpedo Boat No. 1,
Newport, R.I.
April 22, 1890
Inspector of Ordnance.,
In charge of Torpedo Station,
Newport, R.I.

Sir:

In obedience to instructions from the Navy Department, I have the honor to report that I have examined Torpedo Boat No. 1., the "Cushing", and find that the conditions of the contract have been fulfilled except in regard to a distilling apparatus for supplying fresh water for drinking and cooking purposed, which is not on board.

The Boat is now ready for delivery at the Torpedo Station as required by the First Section of said contract.

Very respectfully,
G.A. Converse, Comdr., U.S.N.

Bureau of Ordnance,
Navy Department,
Washington, April 22, 1890

Copy and confirmation of telegram passed this day between Bureau of Ordnance, Navy Department, and the Naval Torpedo Station and War College, Newport, RI.

Turn the bills over to Herreshoff and accept Cushing, if in all respects in accordance with contract, except distilling apparatus.

Copies of correspondence will be sent to you.

Telegraph when vessel has been received.

Naval Torpedo Station and War College,
Newport, R.I.
April 28, 1890.
Subject: Distilling Apparatus of Cushing
Reference No. 720
To: the Chief of the Bureau of Ordnance

Sir:

On April 24th, late in the afternoon, I received the Bureau's telegram of that date in the following words: "Call local members of board on Cushing together, test distilling apparatus on board Cushing as per original instructions and report results."

On the 25th I communicated by telephone with the Herreshoff Manufacturing Company and learned that the distiller was set up and in operation in its shop at Bristol. The President of the Company stated that it was his understanding from his correspondence with the Navy Department that the distiller was to be inspected and tested there.

Accompanied by Lieut. McLean I went to Bristol on the same day and in an interview with the President I declined, in view of my instructions from the Bureau, to make any official inspection of the distiller elsewhere than in its place on board the Cushing but, at his request, I made an examination of the distiller and observed its operation while thus set up in the shop.

The following changes have been made in the apparatus since it was last inspected.

1. The pipe conveying the feed water into the evaporator has been arranged to deliver the water into the bottom of a tinned copper cylinder placed inside of the heating coils from which it overflows into the space containing the coils. Formerly the feed water fell on top of the hot coils and thus promoting priming.
2. A baffle plate has been placed near the top of the cylinder, separating a steam space from the space in which the water is in ebullition, thus securing approximately dry steam to be conveyed into the condensing cylinder.
3. Cocks have been placed in the pipes conveying the steam from the five way cock to the coil in the condensing cylinder, the closing of which when changing either cylinder from an evaporator to a condenser, prevents the entrance of salt water into the condensing coil in case of a possible leak in the five way cock.
4. Water gauges have been placed lower down in the cylinders. By carrying the water level below the upper spires of the coil in the evaporator, the apparatus, operated in the shop, gave excellent, potable water at a rate varying from 20 to 33 gallons an hour, with either cylinder used as the evaporator, the other as the condenser.

The distiller was re-installed in the Cushing on the 26th (Saturday), and was examined by Lieut. McLean and myself today, both while at the wharf and while underway, in the bay. While lying at the wharf, either cylinder used as the evaporator, the other as condenser, gave excellent water, with but a trace of salt when tested with nitrate of silver, at the rate of 18 to 20 gallons per hour. While underway, it was found that when changing the function of a cylinder from evaporating to condensing, a small quantity of oil was at first present in the condensed water, but this disappeared after running the apparatus for a short time. The motion of the boat had no bad effect on the water produced.

We are of the opinion that, with proper attention, the distilling apparatus a now arranged will produce good water for cooking and drinking purposes at the rate of twenty (20) gallons per hour, and we believe it may safely be accepted, subject to the "special reserve" provided for in the eleventh article of the contract.

Respectfully,
Your obedient servant
Thos. F. Jewell, Commander, U.S.N.
Inspector of Ordnance in Charge.
Senior Member of the Board on trial of Cushing.

A Proposal to Strengthen the *Cushing*'s Bow

The following letter from R.C. Smith is dated February 6, 1896:

My dear Comdr. Converse,
The missing and damaged parts of No. 7 torpedo are as follows:

1. Part No. 617 (Screw for removable piece)
2. Part No. 635 (Screws for ball-joint)
3. Part No. 735 (Intermediate gear)

Would the Registered Mail be a suitable way to forward them?

I submitted a plan for strengthening the Cushing's bow, specially the frames which have been bent and weakened, or cracked, to the Bureau of C. & R. [construction and repair], and it has been approved. I am having a copy made with blue print, to send you.

Bryan has been sent to Charleston to inspect the boilers. They were all apart and in no worse condition than last year. The work of bending new tubes had not begun (about 2 weeks ago). Mr. Ward told him the material and workmanship of the boilers, and the care they had received in service, were the best that had ever been brought to his notice.

On February 11, 1896, R.C. Smith writes:

I enclose my letter to C. & R. in regard to Cushing's bow (blue print under separate cover).

As the frames had become weakened and some of them cracked in the web, some strengthening was required, through of course not as much as this plan calls for, it for that purpose only.

On talking the general subject over with the Chief of Bureau, he seemed to think that strengthening the bow might become advisable for other reasons. He instanced the collision of a torpedo boat in the Thames recently when the bow closed up like and accordion, and also spoke of Capt. Wilmots' idea that the bows of the destroyers should be fitted for ramming.

I do not know that I go quite as far as Captain Wilmot, at least at present; but I do believe that their bows should be strong enough to cut into another torpedo boat, or Vedette boat. Under certain circumstances, running down a [illegible word] boat would be the only thing to do.

In a new design, a strengthening in metal alone could be devised at far less cost in weight than the present plan. It would mean some inside plates at the water line and a system of angles and longitudinal with athwartship braces that could be temporarily removed if necessary in order to work in the compartment.

I should be very much pleased if I thought I had your concurrence in these views. I have had some idea of expressing them in a letter to the Secretary, for reference to the Board on Construction. The Board, I think, or perhaps the Secretary himself, would be pretty certain to refer them to you as a beginning.

On Febrary 29, 1896, R.C. Smith writes to the secretary of the U.S. Navy:

Sir:
1. I respectfully forward, under separate cover for the consideration of the Bureau of construction and Repair, a plan for strengthening the bow of the Cushing.
2. The object of this plan, drawn up with the assistance of the Dept. of C. & R. of the Navy Yard, is two-fold; first to strengthen the frames which were recently weakened and in some places cracked by bending in the ice, and second, to strengthen and brace the side of the boat at the water line, both longitudinally and transversely, as a precaution against the same or similar experiences in the future from ice or other causes.
3. The blue print shows very clearly the details of the plan. Generally speaking, it is a system of steel reverse angles, T's, and brace-rods, and an inside wooden sheathing between the frames. The middle of the belt thus formed has been placed at the line of maximum bending of the frames as determined by the recent experience.
4. Spruce is the wood selected on account of its toughness and strength in proportion to its weight. It is recommended that the blocks be dipped in melted paraffin after shaping in order to make them water tight and prevent rotting.
5. The plan shows rosin in the very narrow space forward of the first frame. As it is poured in hot, it affords a simple means of strengthening this part.
6. It is estimated that the total weight of material thus added to the hull is inside of 600 pounds. This is less than the weight of a torpedo, and would not, I think, under the circumstances be a disadvantage.
7. As it has not been found necessary to remove the bow tube to accomplish the present repairs, as was at first thought would be required and which was allowed for

in the estimate, I am of the opinion that the work now recommended can still be done within the original estimates.

On Febrary 14, 1896, G.A. Converse writes to Smith:

My dear Smith:
I have given yours of the 11th February a great deal of thought and consideration, and regret to say that I do not concur with you in the opinions expressed therein; and am sorry that any additional weight is to be put in the bow of the Cushing.

The boat already carries considerable more weight than she was ever intended to carry; and much of it is, in my opinion, unnecessary; and after all the care, trouble and expense incurred in getting the structural weight of the boat as light as possible for the attainment of speed, it seems to me injudicious to add weight, as has been done in this boat from the time she was turned over to the Government. Moreover, I think the object for which she was constructed is being lost sight of. An ice box, another boat, with its davits, etc., etc., have been added, as well as various other appliances; while nothing, to the best of my knowledge and belief, has been taken out. It was never intended that she should be fitted up as a work-shop or carry spare parts for her machinery, as has been done. The addition of 600 pounds at the extreme bow must materially alter the trim, and will be a decided disadvantage in a sea-way by causing the boat to plunge even more deeply than she does now. While it is true, as you say, that the weight is considerably less than that of a torpedo, it differs, inasmuch as it is not portable, and cannot be got rid of in case of an emergency. It is always there, and there it must stay until the boat goes to the bottom.

You must concede that the surroundings in which the Cushing found herself placed at Bordentown were very exceptional; and still, according to all accounts, the boat reached her destination with no other damage than an indented bow.

Regarding the accident which occurred to the English torpedo boat Lightning at the time of her collision with a coal barge: It is not believed that even if the boat's bow had been strengthened as you now propose to strengthen the Cushing's, it would have been able to withstand the shock of such a collision as that seemed to have been, and I think it probable that the longitudinal T irons which you propose to use would have been driven through the water-tight bulkhead and proved of serious danger rather than actual strength.

It should be borne in mind that the Cushing was designed for a *torpedo boat,* and not for a torpedo boat *destroyer*; and that the best authorities abroad recognize that there is a vast difference between the two. I think that in the case of the destroyers it would be well to strengthen the bow sufficiently to enable them to cut down torpedo boats, but not enough to enable them to successfully ram coal barges. Each class of boat should be built for the particular work which it is expected to do; and I do not believe it to be possible to make a light, swift, handy torpedo boat which can be used as gun-boat and ram at will.

Apropos this subject, I have recently recommended, and the Department has approved, the making of the propeller shafts and engine shafts of torpedo boats 6 and

7 [USS *Porter* and USS *Dupont*] hollow, for the express purpose of saving weight. The weight saved will be approximately 7000 pounds, and the cost of saving this weight will be about $2000., or at the rate of nearly 30 cents per pound, and in making this change we are but following foreign practice. Would it not be a little inconsistent for me to recommend the addition of 600 pounds weight to the hull plating to provide for a contingency as remote as that of being required to break ice, when with a few hours notice, and at much less expense, the boat can be strengthened by wood or iron which can be easily removed?

Very truly yours,
G.A. Converse,
Commander, U.S.N.

Outfitting the *Cushing*

List of parts put on board the "Cushing" by the Herreshoff Mfg. Co.

ENGINE ROOM

1- Piston Head socket wrench
1- 1 3/4" Piston Rod Check Wrench.
1- 2" Main Bearing Wrench.
1- Relief Valve Wrench.
1- Wrench for Air Chamber, Cir. pum
3- 1" Connection Rod Wrenches.
2- 3/4" do do
2- 5/8" do do
2- 1/2" do do
2- 7/16" do do
2- 3/8" do do
2- 5/16" do do
2- 1/4" do do
2-3/16" do do

2- spanners, Piston fol. ring.
1- do Wrist Pins.
2- do Check Valve stems.
1- Chain Tongs.
1- 16" Stilson Wrench
1- 10" do do
1- 18" Monkey do
1- 12" do do
1- 8" do do
1- light hammer
1- heavy do
2- Screw Drivers

1- each, 1/2", 7/16", 3/8" 5/16" & 2-1/4" Pins for Stuffing Boxes.
1- Wrench, and Bar for turning Engine over
2- 1/2" screw Handles for lifting cylinder Heads.
2- 10 Gallon Oil Cans
1- 1 Quart measure.
2- Oil lamps.
4- Lanterns.
10- Oil Cups.
1- Pint Measure.
1- Clock.

FIRE ROOM

2- Each, 3/4", 5/8", 7 3/8", Boiler Head Wrenches.
1- Cap Wrench for filling Boilers.
1- 1 1/4" Tube Expander with Machine attachment for same.
1- 1 1/8" do do do

1- Pin for each machine, and 1 Pin & Wrench for hand work.
4- "Moncrief" Water gauge glasses.
4- "Bohemian" do do do
4- Fire Shovels. 2- Slice Bars. 2- Rakes. 2- Fire hooks.
1- Coal filling funnel. 1- Set of Straps for Hoisting Boilers.
2- Brooms. 2- hand brushes.
3- Spare Boiler Tubes for letters A thru J.
Water glasses furnished by Richard & Hewitt, 104 John St. New York.
Pump for Distilling apparatus by Battle Creek Machinery., Co., Battle Creek, Mich.
Boiler Feed Pumps by Worthington, New York.

HULL

18- Life Preservers.	2-Life Rings.
1- 4 1/2" Manila Hawser.	1- Manila running Line.
2- Heaving Lines.	3- Mooring Lines.
2- 9/16" galvanized wire Cables	1- Cable Grip.
1- Spare Tiller.	1- Starboard Lantern
1- Port Lantern.	1- Masthead do
1- Anchor Lantern.	1- Binnacle do
1- Row Boat.	1- Pair Oars. 1- Pair Row-Locks.
1- Rudder.	2- Flag Staffs. 2- Flags.
2- Boat Hooks.	2- Side Steps. 2- Stanchions for same.
1- Galley cook stove.	1- brass Pipe for same.
4- Kettles, 1- Frying Pan	1- Dust Pan, 1- Hand brush.
12- Cushions.	2- Boat Davits, with Blocks and Falls.
1- Anchor Davit with blocks and Fall.	
1- Torpedo davit with chain fall.	
2- Galvanized Anchors.	6- buckets.

April 23, 1890
Subject: Enclosing Certificate of the Inspector of Torpedo Boat No. 1
To: Chief of the Bureau of Ordnance, Navy Department, Washington, D.C.

Sir:

In obedience to the instructions of the Department I have the honor to forward herewith the originals of the certificates of the Inspector of Torpedo Boat No. 1, the Cushing, as to her condition, together with a list of articles on board, when turned over to this Station.

Very respectfully, Your obedient servant
Thos F. Jewell
Commander, U.S.N.

Ten

Observations on Torpedo Boat Trials, Maneuvers, and War Games in Newport

In time of war, the torpedo boat is expected to steal upon a man-of-war in the darkness of night and discharge a torpedo at the superior ship before its presence can be discovered. That such a maneuver could be successfully accomplished was demonstrated in many experiments in Newport, Rhode Island waters. During these experiments—although the man-of-war knew that the torpedo boat was coming and cast her searchlights constantly over the waters—the diminutive torpedo boat got within striking distance before she was discovered.

The effective distance at which a torpedo boat can fire its weapon was estimated at 800 yards, but little accuracy could be expected in the delivery at more than 400 yards. When a capital ship discovers by means of her searchlights the approach of a torpedo boat, all her machine guns pour in a hail of shells on the little craft. But it was not easy, even with a battery of machine guns, to hit so small a target as a torpedo boat going at the rate of 35 mph, seen suddenly for an instant in the glare of the searchlight.

The *Cushing*

One of the most satisfactory of the new additions to the United States Navy is the torpedo boat *Cushing*. This boat lately sailed from Rhode Island, where she was built, to Washington. The little ship is satisfactory as a first example, and shows that the government can, and has, after long trial, produced one torpedo boat that is nearly up to the best standards of its class.

The *Cushing* lately sailed from Newport to New York, driven at the highest speed they could get from her, and made the voyage in three minutes less than seven hours, at an average velocity of 19 1/2 knots per hour. This is superior performance, and indicates an excellence of construction in the mechanism and vessel that is very promising for the future.

Economy of space was one of the chief objects in view on the part of her builders. Every cubic foot is utilized. She has eleven compartments and ten water-tight bulkheads. There are no doors connecting the compartments. The lower decks fore and aft are entered only by hatchways. She has fuel bunkers all along her sides, abreast of her engines. Her only other protection is her pumping machinery. She can

On board a torpedo boat under a destroyer's searchlight. (Drawing by Fred T. Jane, 1895.)

pump 100 tons of water in seven minutes, 870 tons per hour, and her own weight in less than ten minutes. If she should have a shot hole nine inches in diameter through her engine room compartment, her pumping capacity would enable her to keep free from water.

When equipped, she will carry a torpedo tube on each bow and a torpedo gun amidships, and will thus be able to launch three torpedoes at once. She will carry five rapid-fire one-pounder cannons, and will have a search light.

The success of the *Cushing* and her presence in Washington, where members of Congress can witness her maneuvers, will, we hope, lead them to authorize the construction without delay of a better and faster class, such, for example, as the flock of torpedo boats possessed by the Italian government. [*Scientific American*, May 10, 1890.]

Search Lights and Torpedo Boats

A test of the value of search lights for naval purposes was lately made at the naval station, Newport, Rhode Island. It was arranged that during the evening of the 15th inst. the torpedo boats *Cushing* and *Stiletto* should endeavor to enter the harbor while search lights should be employed in detecting them if possible.

The *Cushing* was painted nearly a black, while the *Stiletto* was left a dark green. The test took place at 9:30 in the evening. The boats entered the range of the search light and padded to their anchorage while the officers were still looking for them at the entrance to the bay, for ten minutes the boats were in the open channel, but the deep color of the vessels blended with the color of the rocky shores so they were not detected.

A torpedo boat passing a battleship in a rough seaway. (Drawing by Fred T. Jane, 1895.)

In general, the search lights may be depended upon to show up the presence of vessels at a distance, but in this case there was a failure. [*Scientific American,* May 26, 1894.]

Search Lights in Naval Warfare

As torpedo boats and their destroyers must often rely upon darkness to cover their operations, it is of the first importance that means should be employed to discover their movements. Hence has come into use the electric search light.

Inasmuch as a ship finds her way across the sea by faith rather than by sight, she does not need out-door illumination except when coming into harbor and making her wharf. Under such circumstances at night it is particularly helpful to the pilot, in finding channel-buoys and picking out his slip, to be able to use a powerful arc light.

But the chief use to which this apparatus is put by war-ships is detection of torpedo boats. Not only do these small craft have little superstructure, but they are painted to look like the sea—dark gray, dark green, or a kindred hue. Germany prefers a bluish-gray for her torpedo boats, and France a leaden color. The latter tint was used on the *Almirante Condell* and *Almirante Lynch* in the Chilean Civil War, when these boats entered the harbor of Iquique unperceived. In 1894, when the American torpedo boats *Stiletto* and *Cushing* tried, successfully, to enter Newport harbor without detection by the naval officers keeping watch with the aid of search-lights, those vessels were almost black, having previously worn an olive-green coat. [Young, James Rankin. *War with Spain,* 1898.]

A battleship crew operating under a ship-mounted searchlight scans the moonless Newport Harbor in vain for the stealthily approaching torpedo boat. The Naval Torpedo Station at Newport was the cutting edge of electrical technology, not only for its weapons but for electric equipment used aboard ships.

A torpedo boat using her searchlight during a night operation.

Search Light Practice in Newport, Rhode Island

Rules were arranged similar to those which have governed the drill between the torpedo station and the *Cushing,* except that Lieut. Smith promised not to take shelter behind any obstructions within 2000 yards—one sea mile—despite the fact that the battleship *Maine* has four searchlights and should consequently be impregnable against torpedo attack, if there is such a possibility with reliance on search lights alone, without their scouts.

The officers of the ship thought they were sure of success in such an attack, and in a harbor where they had but four narrow channels to sweep and a search light to each. But they were doomed to disappointment, as the torpedo boat had an easy task.

November 22 – The *Cushing* ran out to the ship in mid-harbor under running lights. After a brief conference these lights were hidden, and the *Cushing* sped off toward the channel. The search lights swept the waters, but the boat was not to be seen. She had doubled her tracks, passed within 1500 yards of the ship, and run out to sea. Then she glided up the channel, close under Fort Adams' shore, and then laid out a direct course for the ship. She was discovered only when within twenty seconds of torpedoing distance, and before all the lights could be trained upon her, to say nothing of the effective battery, she had discharged all three of her rockets. When the allotted two minutes had expired after her discovery she was alongside the ship. The second attack, while differing in method, was equally successful for the *Cushing.* [*Scientific American,* December 7, 1895.]

Official Navy Report of the *Cushing*'s Attacks under Search Light
U.S. Torpedo Boat Cushing
Navy Yard, Washington, D.C
23 December, 1895
[To] Commander G.A. Converse, U.S.N.
President, Naval Torpedo Board

Sir:
1. I submit herewith a summary of the exercises which have taken place during the season between the Cushing and the search-lights at the Torpedo Station or aboard ship. The results of these exercises have all been separately reported at the time of their occurrence.
2. At the start there were no rules governing the attacks, except that the Cushing was to reach an extreme torpedo range of 800 yards before discovery in order to be successful.
3. Six attacks in all were made under the above conditions, one on the 9th of September, two on the 9th of October, and three on the 10th of October.
4. There was no moon on any of these occasions and the nights were generally fair to clear and dark.
5. The results were as follows:

1st. attack, Cushing reached 200 yards without discovery.
2nd. attack, Cushing reached 300 to 200 yards without discovery.
3rd. attack, Cushing reached 1000 yards when discovered.
4th. attack Cushing reached 400 yards without discovery.
5th. attack Cushing reached 800 to 700 yards when discovered
6th. attack, Cushing reached 1000 yards when discovered.
Four of the six attacks were therefore successful.

6. The speed of these attacks varies from 10 to 15 knots. The boat was often in the beam of the light within a distance at which it seemed that she must be discovered.
7. There was a marked improvement noticeable in the skill of the observers in sweeping and in recognizing the boat when the beam came on. In the later attacks the distance of discovery was generally greater.
8. At this stage it became apparent that a set of rules and signals would be desirable in order to prevent mistakes in times and distances and to liken the exercises as much as possible to the conditions of a real attack. The Board appointed by you therefore formulated the rules which, with slight changes, have been subsequently used. The signals made are simple and easy to understand, and by always having a second pistol ready in regard to times or distances.
9. Under the rules the Cushing made six attacks on the Station search-light and two on the U.S.S. Maine. After two attacks on the Station, the arc of approach was; limited to 65° in order to give the single light that was used a smaller sector to cover. After the next two attacks the time limit was reduced from, 2 1/2 to 2 minutes. There were no subsequent changes to the rules.

10. Under the rules, the 5th attack failed by 6 seconds. The others [7] were successful. The Cushing in the [8] attacks made use of no cover within a radius of 2000 yards.

Very respectfully,
R.C. Smith, Lieut., U.S.N., Commanding.

Endorsement of Search Light Exercises
Torpedo Station,
Newport, R.I.
Jan. 18 1896.
Respectfully forwarded for the information of the Bureau of Ordnance.

1. It is desirable that advantage be taken of every available opportunity for making torpedo boat attacks on vessels of the Navy in commission for the purpose of exercising the crews of the ships in the use of the search-light.
2. Practice causes a wonderful improvement in the handling of the lights and in the ability of the observers to recognize objects; and it will be of inestimable value to the officers in charge of the boats in enabling them to determine the best methods of maneuvering in order to avoid detection.

G.A. Converse, Commander, U.S.N.
President, Naval Torpedo Board

The New Torpedo Boats

A second triple addition to the mosquito fleet of the United States Navy has been provided for in the act of Congress of March 2, 1895, appropriating for the construction of torpedo boats Nos. 6, 7 (*Porter* and *Dupont*), and 8 (the *Ericsson*), the individual cost of which, including governmental superintendence, preparation of plans, and the provision and installation of ordnance outfit must not exceed $175,000—a moderate allowance, which, but for present prices and skillful management of design, would be impracticable.

With a displacement of 180 tons, they will be 170 feet between perpendiculars, with an extreme water line beam of 17 feet upon the mean, normal draught of 5 feet 6 inches. The hulls are models of the most recent practice; with an easy razor-like entrance and a long fine run below water toward the screws. The "tumble-home," which begins just forward of the midship section, increases afterward, where it broadens out over the propellers, giving a very full water line area of shallow draught. The flat form of the stern prevents the settling so common to torpedo boats under full power, while holding to the water in all conditions of weather and preventing racing of the screws.

So important is speed in this type of craft that fifty percent of the total displacement will be absorbed by the boilers, engines and appurtenances, and the magnitude of this amount may best be appreciated when it is know that this allowance is just double that for the motive mechanism of the commerce destroyers *Columbia* and *Minneapolis*.

The engines, which are of the triple expansion sort, each in its own water-tight compartment and actuating a separate screw, are very fine examples of power and compactness, beautifully balanced, with a very nice distribution and division of weights. With a common stroke of 18 inches, impelled by steam at a pressure of 250 pounds to the square inch, supplied by three water tube boilers that flank the engine space—two forward and one aft—the two 6 foot manganese bronze screws will be driven by the engines at the rate of 395 turns-a-minute, developing an indicated horse power of 3,200 and driving the boats through the water at a speed of 23 knots an hour. The normal coal supply will be 12 tons, with a total bunker capacity of 60.

There will be no search lights, but the boats will be lighted by electricity, and natural ventilation will be ample to insure comfort under all conditions of service. Folding boats will be carried.

The officers will be aft, while the crew will be provided for in the forecastle and just below on the berth deck. Excepting the captain and engineer, who will have separate state rooms, and bunks, the two other officers, the four machinists, and the sixteen seamen, each in a common country, will sleep in folding berths, easily turned out of the way to afford added space and comfort when not in use.

No premiums are offered for increased speed need not be feared; when even a more excellent performance may reasonably be hoped for.

One boat will be built by Moran Brothers company, of Seattle, Washington, for $163,350, and the two others will be built by Herreshoff Manufacturing Company, of Bristol, R.I. for $144,000 apiece. [*Scientific American,* January 18, 1896.]

Torpedo Boat Armament

The boats will be built of steel (No. 6, the *Porter;* No. 7, the *Dupont* and No. 8, the *Ericsson*). The armament will consist of three 18 inch torpedo tubes on swivel mounts and of four 1 pounder rapid-fire guns. Six hundred rounds of ammunition will be allowed for the guns, while four automobile torpedoes—the type yet undetermined—will be provided; the spare one being carried in a steel storage case on the starboard beam. The torpedo discharges will be arranged on the main deck, two forward and one aft, the forward tubes being placed slightly "en echelon," admitting of considerable athwartship fire in addition to the extended field of action of each on its own side. The after discharge will be on the center line, and will have an unhampered sweep of 280 degrees. This emplacement is devoid of "dead angles," and give an all-around discharge of great scope.

The conning towers, of which there are two, will be near the bow and the stern, each about 35 feet from its respective end. Hand steering gear will supplement in the forward tower the steam mechanism common to both towers, affording one more chance in case of mechanical failure.

The forward tower will be surmounted by one of the 1 pounder guns, to be worked from a gallery on the after side. The three others will be mounted along the sides, two on the port and one on the starboard.

The coast defense torpedo boat MacKenzie.

The freeboard forward is carried up to a height of 12 feet 6 inches, adding materially to the sea-going qualities of the boats while yielding increased berthing space for the crew and a housing for some of the forward mechanisms. [*Scientific American,* January 18, 1896.]

The *Porter*'s Trial Run

Torpedo boat No. 6, (the *Porter*) which has just been completed by the Herreshoffs, was sent on a preliminary trial run by her builders on January 20, when she made a speed of 26.85 knots. The result was very gratifying to the firm, considering the circumstances of the trial; for the run was made with an untrained crew in the engine room and under reduced boiler pressure. The contract calls for a speed of 27 1/2 knots under 220 pounds of steam, and as the little craft was carrying only 180 pounds to the square inch, it was confidently believed that under the favorable conditions of a trial trip 28 knots an hour will be realized. The water was fairly smooth, the breeze blowing across the course, which was a part of that which has been laid out for the official trial. The expectations based upon this performance were realized in another builders' trial, on February 5, during which, in a series of eight runs over the measured mile course in Narragansett Bay, she averaged 28.76 knots an hour. Her highest speed was 30.1 knots, and every mile was run off at a higher speed than the contract calls for, viz., 27 1/2 knots. The steam pressure ranged from 205 to 225 pounds to the square inch, the latter being the maximum allowed. [*Scientific American,* March 6, 1897.]

The Torpedo Boat *Porter*

The accompanying illustration [page 63], showing the little craft in dry dock No. 2, at the Brooklyn navy yard, will give the reader some idea of the beautiful lines upon which the hull of this fleet vessel is modeled. It will be noticed that the water line

The torpedo boats Porter *(left) and the* Thornton in a period photo postcard.

shows a draft of about four feet at the bow, but when the boat is being driven at its full speed of nearly 29 knots an hour, it settles at the stern and lifts its forefoot clear of the water to such an extent that five or six feet of the keel is visible. This is a common occurrence when the smaller class of light draft torpedo boat destroyers and pleasure yachts are driven at speeds in the neighborhood of 30 knots an hour.

Owing to the altitude from which the photograph was taken, we get an excellent idea of the arrangement of the deck. It will be noticed that a turtle back deck extends from the bow aft as far as the rear of the forward conning tower. This is intended to give the boat increased buoyancy when she is running against a head sea. Just forward of the conning tower is a one-pounder rapid fire gun on a tripod mount. Two other one-pounder guns on similar mounts are located on either beam on the after part of the deck. The long cylindrical object seen on the port side of the boat in front of the forward funnel is a torpedo launching tube. There is another one amidships on the starboard side, and a third tube is located at the stern on the center line. The launching tube is nothing more nor less than a gun, of which the torpedo is the projectile. The latter, loaded with its charge of explosive, and with its air reservoir charged with compressed air, is thrust into the gun, or tube, at the breech- the breech block is then closed and the torpedo is ejected by firing a small charge of powder or releasing a charge of compressed air. The launching tube is carried upon a central pivot mount, and may be elevated or depressed in the same way as an ordinary gun.

David Dixon Porter.

In making an attack, the torpedo boat would charge upon the ship at full speed, and when she was within torpedo range she would swing round to port or starboard so as to bring her launching tubes to bear. If the bow torpedo or that amidships failed to reach the mark, she would have another chance with the tube that is located at her stern.

As the *Porter* is built of the very thinnest kind of plating, she would be penetrable by the smallest rapid fire guns of the enemy, and the mad charge through the hail of bullets and shells that would be rained upon her would evidently be somewhat of the nature of a forlorn hope. However, it is not likely that torpedo boat attack will often be carried out in broad daylight. The best work of these little boats will be done on dark nights and in foggy weather; and even if they never strike a blow, the moral effect which they will exercise upon the enemy will be well worth the cost of their construction and maintenance. [*Scientific American,* May 22, 1897.]

Torpedo Practice at Newport

Although torpedo warfare has not yet achieved results at all proportionate to the amount of thought and skill that have been devoted to it, the failure has probably been due more to lack of opportunity or inefficient handling than to any deficiency in the torpedo itself.

Torpedo practice. The Morris *launches an 18-inch Whitehead torpedo in Newport. (From* Scientific American, *March 10, 1900.)*

The illustration which we present here with is one of the best instantaneous photographs of the discharge of a torpedo that has ever come under our notice. The view [above] was taken from astern of the torpedo boat *Morris,* just at the instant she fired an 18-inch Whitehead torpedo from her starboard broadside tube. As most of our readers are aware, the torpedo is nothing more nor less than a small, cigar-shaped submarine vessel, whose interior is divided transversely into six chambers.

The torpedo is "launched" by firing it from a gun in the shape of a cylindrical tube, into which the torpedo is thrust from the rear through a breech mechanism, which is approximately similar to that used in artillery. It is ejected by the explosion of a small charge of gunpowder, which compresses the air surrounding the rear half of the torpedo and thrusts it out of the tube without any serious jar. As it is driven out a catch on the launching tube serves to open the throttle between the compressed air chamber and the engine; and with her propellers revolving at an enormous speed the little submarine craft takes its dive, as shown in our illustration, into the water. When it first enters, the torpedo falls below the normal plane at which it is designed to travel, but the action of the pendulum in the secret chamber throws up a pair of horizontal rudders at the stern and causes the little craft to return towards the surface. The first part of its run is thus made on a wave line which crosses and recrosses the desired and ultimate level of submersion. The piston and the pendulum in the secret chamber gradually bring the torpedo to its true course.

Commonly the United States torpedoes [torpedo boats] carry three charges [weapons]; one on either beam and another astern. The starboard and the astern launching tubes will be noticed in the illustration. [*Scientific American,* March 10, 1900.]

Accident to the *Dupont* at Newport

If one were in search of ocular evidence of the fine quality of steel which is used in the construction of torpedo boats, he could not do better than study the crumpled up bow of the torpedo boat *Dupont,* as shown in the accompanying illustration. It will be seen that the plating has been folded back on itself, concertina-fashion, so that the whole of the forward compartment, which was about 8 feet in length, has been compressed within a space of not more than 2 or 3 feet. This was an extemporized "cold-bending test" that speaks well for the quality of the material. Not only does the mild, open-hearth, steel, of which the thin 1/8-inch plates are composed, fail to show a single crack in any of the folds or laminations, but the riveted joints of the plating in many cases are not even started. The accident to the *Dupont* happened at Newport when the craft was being brought into her berth. Ordinarily in bringing these little

The Dupont*'s crumpled bow. This view shows the damage done to the* Dupont *after her collision with the Newport torpedo station dock. (Photograph by F.H. Child; courtesy* Scientific American.*)*

Inspection of the Dupont. *Navy inspectors survey the damaged bow of the* Dupont. *(Courtesy* Scientific American.*)*

craft to their moorings, they are run into the dock at a speed of from 10 to 12 knots, and when a given point on the vessel passes the end of the dock the bell is rung for full speed astern. Such is the power of the engines that the craft is brought to rest as soon as the stern has passed within the pier head. On this particular occasion the signal was given about a second too late, with the result that the *Dupont* struck the end of the dock when she was yet traveling about four knots an hour. As it happened, the bow served as an excellent buffer, bringing the vessel gradually to a rest without dislocating the steampipes, boilers or engine fittings. It is a remarkable fact that, although the crumpling of the bow extended to the first watertight bulkhead, the latter remained practically watertight, and the little vessel, had she been at sea, would have made the trip to her dock with safety. [*Scientific American,* July 28, 1900.]

Eleven

The Herreshoffs' Other Government Contracts

As noted previously in this book, the Herreshoff brothers decided to stop selling their boats to the U.S. government after delivery of the *Gwin* in 1898. The government, however, did not stop buying Herreshoff boats.

Over a period of about seven months in the 1917–1918 period, the Herreshoffs delivered at least six boats to various private owners. Those individuals in turn sold or leased their boats to the U.S. Navy. These are listed and described in the following paragraphs, taken from navy records.

1. HULL No. 306: STEEL-HULLED PATROL BOAT; weight, 60 tons; length, 112'5' beam, 15'2"; draft, 4'; speed, 24 knots; armament, one 6-pound gun. In 1917, Hull No. 306 was contracted by Alfred DuPont of Wilmington, Delaware, at the urging of Assistant Secretary of the Navy Franklin D. Roosevelt, with the intention of later allowing her to be bought by the Navy. Hull No. 306 was purchased by the Navy, taken over on February 14, 1918, and commissioned February 27, 1918, at Newport, Rhode Island.

The patrol boat was first taken to New London, Connecticut, in company with two other Herreshoff-built vessels (Hull Nos. 308 and 321), to be fitted with listening gear. She subsequently sailed on May 5, 1918, for the Canal Zone, where she assumed duty as a harbor patrol vessel. She continued to perform this duty until the end of World War I, after which she served the 15th Naval District as a patrol craft. The boat was then loaned to the War Department in October 1920 for use by the Army Air Service in the Canal Zone. She was returned to the Navy in March 1921, and was taken to Philadelphia and placed on sale, finally being purchased by W.A.D. Smith of New York City, on December 1, 1922.

2. No. 308: STEEL-HULLED PATROL BOAT; weight, 60 tons, length 112'5"; beam, 15'2 draft, 4'; speed, 24 knots; armament, one 6-pound gun. Hull No. 308 was contracted in 1917, by R.E. Todd, of New York City, who asked Secretary Roosevelt how he might contribute to the war effort. He was told that he might have a boat built for later sale to the Navy. Herreshoff No. 308 was accordingly bought by the Navy, and commissioned at Newport on February 23, 1918.

After spending a short time at New London, Connecticut, and fitted out with listening gear, the craft sailed for the Canal Zone, stopping with her two companions at Charleston, South Carolina; Key West, Florida; and Guantanamo, Cuba. She

The Herreshoff-built steam launch Lagoda. (*From* U.S. Navy from the Revolution to Date.)

arrived at Christobal on June 1, 1918, and began duty as a patrol vessel. For the next two years she was engaged in patrolling at Balboa and Colon, in the U.S. Canal Zone. Later, she was loaned to the Governor of the Canal Zone, and returned to U.S. Navy custody in September 1923. She was stricken from the Navy's list of active ships on September 12, 1923, and sold to J.A. Kenny, Brooklyn, N.Y., May 27, 1924.

3. No. 309: MOTOR PATROL BOAT; weight, 25 tons; length, 12'6"; draft, 3'6"; speed, 17 knots; armament, one 3-pound, and one 1-pound gun.

Hull No. 309 was designed and built for government use by the Herreshoff Manufacturing Company, in 1917, and leased by the Navy from her owner, Winthrop W. Aldrich of Newport Rhode Island. She was taken over by the Navy on October 26, 1917, and commissioned November 15.

This particular motor boat was assigned to the 2nd Naval District, based in Newport, and she was assigned section patrol duties off Block Island and in Narragansett Bay. She was returned to her owner December 31, 1918.

4. HULL No. 313, WOODEN YACHT, was ordered, delivered, and assigned to the 1st Naval District, Boston, on October 6, 1917. She was not taken over by the Navy, and apparently saw no service.

5. HULL No. 321: A STEEL-HULLED SUB-CHASER; weight, 60 tons; length, 112'5"; beam, 15'2"; draft, 4'; speed, 24 knots; armament, one 6-pound gun.

This boat was built for Payne Whitney of New York, who had inquired of Secretary Roosevelt what he might do for the war effort, and it was suggested that he might contract the Herreshoff Manufacturing Company to build a subchaser that could be later purchased by the Navy. Hull No. 321 was taken over and commissioned March 24, 1918, at Newport.

The 82-foot Herreshoff-built Wave *was put into service in 1892. She carried workers from the government landing in Newport to the torpedo station on Goat Island. (U.S. Navy photograph.)*

After listening gear was installed at the Navy's Underwater Sound Laboratory New London, Connecticut, she sailed for Cristobal, Canal Zone, arriving on June 1, 1918. She was assigned duty as a patrol vessel in Panama Bay and was used for aerial patrol off Panama. After first being offered for sale, the motor boat was designated for duty at the Naval Torpedo Station, Keyport, Washington. While being towed to Washington on October 7, 1921, the towing hawser parted and before the towing vessel, could make her fast again, the boat sank. The sinking occurred off the coast of southern California.

6. HULL No. 322: STEEL MOTOR BOAT; weight, 40 tons; length, 83'4"; beam, 12'8"; draft, 3'; speed, 26 knots; armament, one 3-pound and one 1-pound gun.

This craft was built to government specifications. She was originally contracted for by H.V. Morgan of Philadelphia, on the understanding that she would be later purchased by the Navy. She was taken over on March 22, 1918, at Newport and commissioned April 2, 1918.

After a brief period of outfitting and training, Hull No. 322 was assigned to the 3rd Naval District as a patrol craft. She operated during World War I and after in Ambrose Channel, East River, and Long Island Sound as a patrol boat, until being withdrawn from active service and laid up at Marine Basin on August 28, 1919. Subsequently, Hull No. 322 was loaned to the Dock Department of New York City; but she was found too large to be economically operated and so was returned to the Navy on November 19, 1920, and on July 18, 1921 she was sold to W. Lindberg of Birmingham, Alabama.

7. HULL No. 323: MOTOR BOAT; weight, 60 tons; length, 112'5"; beam, 15'2"; draft, 4'; speed, 24 knots; armament, one 6-pound gun.

Herreshoff Hull No. 306 in Bristol Harbor. No. 306 is seen here with government inspectors aboard. (U.S. Navy photograph.)

This vessel was built according to government plans; she was contracted for by J.P. Morgan of New York City. Morgan had this boat built under an agreement with Secretary Roosevelt that upon completion the Navy would buy or lease. She was acquired by the Navy from Morgan on June 6, 1918, and commissioned June 15, 1918, at Newport.

After being outfitted at New London, Connecticut, she was assigned to the 1st Naval District, Boston, for duty as section patrol boat. Based at Boston, she operated as a patrol craft off Nantucket Island and in Boston Harbor, until transferred to the 2nd Naval District temporarily in December 1918. Herreshoff Hull No. 323 was later transferred back to Boston and in December 1920, was assigned as a general purpose craft at the Naval Torpedo Station, Alexandria, Virginia. She remained on this duty until July 10, 1923, when she was transferred to the Naval Torpedo Station, Newport, for patrol and dispatch duty. She was declaimed surplus and sold on May 3, 1927.

The preceding entries represent some of the Herreshoff Manufacturing Company's additional vessels in the service of the U.S. Navy and serve as an additional historic entry to the long life of the Herreshoffs in supporting the federal government and its navy.

HERRESHOFF CONTRACTS WITH THE U.S. GOVERNMENT

Owner	Length (Type)	Date	Name of Boat
U.S. Navy	28' (Steam Cutter)	1879	*Dolphin*
U.S. Navy	100'	1879	*Inca*
U.S. Navy	42' (Open Launch)	1880	*Spray*
U.S. Navy	57' (Spar Torpedo Boat)	1881	*Lightning*
U.S. Navy	94'	1884	*Lucele*
U.S. Navy	138' (Torpedo boat)	1890	*Cushing*
U.S. Coast Survey	23' (Tender)	1892	*Wasp*
U.S. Navy	28' (Steam Launch)	1893	*Enterprise*
U.S. Coast Survey	28'	1895	*Eagle*
U.S. Navy	175'6" (Torpedo Boat)	1897	*Dupont*
U.S. Navy	175'6" (Torpedo Boat)	1897	*Porter*
U.S. Navy	100' (Torpedo Boat)	1898	*Gwin*
U.S. Navy	140' (Torpedo Boat)	1898	*Morris*
U.S. Navy	100' (Torpedo Boat)	1898	*Talbot*
U.S. Navy	33' (Steam Launch)	1899	*Atalanta*
U.S. Navy	40' (Rescue Boat)	1890	
U.S. Navy	83' (Ferryboat)	1892	*Wave*
U.S. Navy	54'3" (Cabin Yacht)	1896	*Javelin*
U.S. Coast Survey	26'	1900	*Yankton*
U.S. Navy	(Ten 58' Steal Barges)	1902	
U.S. Navy	(Ten F5 Flying Boat Hulls)	1902	
U.S. Navy	(Ten H16 Flying Boat Hulls)	1902	
U.S. Navy	(Seaplane)	1902	N.C.1
U.S. Coast Survey	27'	1903	*Patterson*
U.S. Navy	29'5 1/2" (Steam Launch for the USS *Chicago*)	1903	*Lagoda*
U.S. Navy	40' (Five Gasoline Launches used as Torpedo Retrievers)	1905	C365-C369
U.S. Fish Commission	26'3"	1909	*Albatross*
U.S. Navy	30'	1914	*Vixen*
U.S. Army	45'	1929	*Kanawa*
U.S. Coast Survey	28'	1932	*Yosemite*

Herreshoff Hull No. 309. This class was designed and built expressly for patrol service in World War I. (U.S. Navy photograph.)

Herreshoff Hull No. 306 revving her engines at the boatyard's piers in Bristol, Rhode Island. (U.S. Navy photograph.)

Twelve

The Authorization of Torpedo Boats and Improvements to the Naval Torpedo Station

THE NAVAL TORPEDO STATION

The Native American name for Goat Island, the site of the Naval Torpedo Station at Newport, was *Nante Simunka.* The City of Newport purchased the island in 1676 and requested the English crown to fortify it. In 1703, four acres were reserved for fortifications and the remaining six acres were plotted for house lots.

In the century that followed, the island fort was known as Fort Anne. During the American Revolution, it was Fort George in honor of Gen. George Washington. When the torpedo station occupied the site, it became Fort Walcott. In 1799, the federal government bought the island from the City of Newport and put it under the jurisdiction of the U.S. War Department. For the next 70 years, the island operated under federal control as an activity of the army.

The U.S. Navy's initial interest in Goat Island came during the Civil War, when the Naval Academy was moved, temporarily, from Annapolis. The U.S. War Department loaned the island to the navy, and temporary classrooms were built adjacent to Fort Walcott. The navy formally took over the island in 1869 with the establishment of the first torpedo station. The site was transferred to the navy under a long-term lease for an annual rental of $5,000. Lt. Comdr. E.O. Matthews was designated first commanding officer and inspector of ordnance in charge.

The new activity's broad mission was to function as both an experimental station and a school in a wide range of areas, including the following: stationary torpedoes (moored mines) of all types; spar and towed torpedoes, including design, development, and fleet use; automobile torpedoes; design, development, and production of fuses, explosives, and warheads; and electricity and electrical devices, including fuses, batteries, lighting systems, generators, and wire-guided torpedoes.

The physical plant at the Newport torpedo station continued to expand during the 1890s as the seawall was extended 1,600 feet across the mud flats to the lighthouse on the

Piles being driven for new torpedo boat piers on the east side of the Naval Torpedo Station at Newport, c. 1915. Note the torpedo boats docked at right. (Courtesy Naval War College Museum, Newport.)

The Naval Torpedo Station at Newport, April 5, 1934. This view, looking south, shows the progress of work on new bulkhead near yard craft piers. (Courtesy Naval War College Museum, Newport.)

northern tip of the island. Cinders from the island's powerhouse were used to fill in the flats; as they disappeared, the size of the island steadily increased.

ACT March 2, 1891: Under the Bureau of Equipment

Equipment of New Ships of the Navy: supplying anchors, chain cables, galley and fixtures, standing and running rigging, sails, awnings, and other canvas work, and other articles comprising the equipment outfit of ships, according to their type, namely: Protected cruisers numbered seven, eight, nine, ten, eleven, and twelve; the Monterey; gunboats numbered five and six; the harbor-defense vessel known as the Ammen ram; ironclads Puritan, Terror, Amphirite, and Monadnock; the steel practice cruiser provided for by the act of September seventh, eighteen hundred and eighty-eight, and the torpedo cruiser and torpedo boat authorized by the act of June thirteenth, eighteen hundred and ninety, four hundred thousand dollars.

Bureau of Ordnance: Torpedo Station, Newport, Rhode Island

For necessary repairs to ordnance buildings, magazines, gun parks, boats, lighters, wharves, machinery, and other objects of the like character, thirty thousand dollars.

For labor, material, freight, and express charges; general care of and repairs to grounds, buildings and wharves; boats, instruction, instruments, tools, furniture, experiments and general torpedo outfits, sixty thousand dollars.

In general storehouse: One clerk, at one thousand two hundred dollars.

ACT March 3, 1893: Under the Bureau of Ordnance

Submarine Torpedo Boat

For building a submarine torpedo boat and conducting experiments therewith, two hundred thousand dollars, to be taken from the balances of appropriations on hand July first eighteen hundred and ninety-three, to the credit of armor and armament of vessels heretofore authorized.

Naval torpedo Station, Newport, Rhode Island

For one chemist, at two thousand five hundred dollars; one clerk, at one thousand two hundred dollars; one draftsman, at one thousand five hundred dollars. In all, twenty-six thousand eight hundred and twenty-four dollars; and no other fund appropriated by this act shall be used to payment for such service.

ACT July 26, 1894: Under the Bureau of Ordnance

Increase of the Navy: Construction and Steam Machinery:

The Secretary of the Navy is hereby authorized to use the four hundred and fifty thousand dollars "for construction of one additional cruiser of the Vesuvius type," appropriated by this Act of March second, eighteen hundred and eighty-nine, or so much thereof as may be necessary for the construction, armament, and equipment of three torpedo boats, to cost, all together, not more than the said sum of four hundred and fifty thousand dollars.

ACT June 10, 1896: Under the Bureau of Ordnance

Increase of the Navy

. . . three torpedo boats, to have a maximum speed of not less than thirty knots, to cost in all not exceeding eight hundred thousand dollars; and not to exceed ten torpedo boats to cost in all not exceeding five hundred thousand dollars, and to have the highest practicable speed for vessels of their class; and not more than two of said battleships and not more than three of said torpedo boats shall be built in one yard or by one contracting party, and in each case the contract shall be awarded by the Secretary of the Navy to the lowest best responsible bidder; and in the construction of all said vessels all of the provisions of the Act of August third, eighteen hundred and eighty-six, entitled "An Act to increase the naval establishment."

ACT May 4, 1898: Under the Bureau of Ordnance
Increase of the Navy

. . . and sixteen torpedo boat destroyers of about four hundred tons displacement, and twelve torpedo boats of about one hundred and fifty tons displacement, to have the highest practicable speed, and to cost in all, exclusive of armament, not exceeding six million nine hundred thousand dollars; and one gunboat to take the place of the United States steamship Michigan. . . .

. . . and not more than five of said torpedo boat destroyers, and not more than four of said torpedo boats shall be built in one yard or by one contraction party.

The Naval Torpedo Station at Newport, Goat Island, 1945. By the end of World War II, a total of 5,594 Mark 14 submarine-launched torpedoes, nearly 6,000 Mark 15 destroyer-launched torpedoes, and hundreds of Mark 13 aircraft-launched torpedoes were artisan-made at the station.

The Naval Torpedo Station at Newport, Goat Island, c. mid-1930s. Gould Island is visible in the center background. During the years shortly before the start of World War II, three new classes of improved navy destroyers having twin deck mounts of multiple torpedo tubes began entering the fleet.

The physical plant at the torpedo station continued to expand during the 1890s as the seawall was extended 1,600 feet across the mud flats to the lighthouse on the northern tip of the island. Cinders from the island's powerhouse were used to fill in the flats; as they disappeared, the size of the island steadily increased.

Statistical Records of U.S. Torpedo Boats Built between 1886 and 1898

Performances of the torpedo boats *Farragut* built by the Union Iron Works, San Francisco, and the *Davis,* built by Wolff & Zwicker, Portland, Ore., in exceeding on their trial runs the stipulated contract speed, having directed attention to the showing made by the other torpedo boats of the United States Navy. The records of the torpedo boats thus far accepted are as follows:

ull No.	NAME	BUILDER	DATE Purchase	Trial Speed	Contract Speed	TONS	Draft Ft. In.	Length Ft. In.	COST	GUNS	TORP Whitehead	Off.	Men
1	CUSHING	Herreshoff	1886	22.50	22.00	58	4.11	138.75	82,750	3, 6 pdr	3, 18"	2	20
2	ERICSSON	Iowa Iron	1894	24.00	24.00	120	4.9	149.50	113,500	4, 1 pdr	3, 18"		
3	FOOTE	Columbian	1894	24.53	24.54	142	5.0	160.00	97,500	3,1 pdr	2, 18"	2	26
4	ROGERS	Columbian	1894	24.49	24.50	142	5.0	150.00	97,500	3, 1 pdr	2, 18"	2	36
5	WINSLOW	Columbian	1894	24.82	24.50	142	5.0	160.00	97,500	3, 1 pdr	3, 18"	2	30
6	PORTER	Herreshoff	1895	28.63	29.00	165	4.8	175.00		3, 1 pdr	3, 18"	2	30
7	DUPONT	Herreshoff	1895	28.58	27.50	165	4.8	175.00	144,000	4, 1 pdr	3, 18"	2	30
8	ROWAN	Moran Bros	1895	27.07	26.00	210	5.11	170.00		4, 1 pdr	2, 18"	2	36
9	DAHLGRIN	Bath Iron	1896	30.00	30.00	146	4.7	147.00		4, 1 pdr	2, 18"	2	26
10	CRAVEN	Bath Iron	1896	30.00	31.00	146	4.7	147.00		4, 1 pdr	2, 18"	2	26
11	FARRAGUT	Union Iron	1896	30.13	30.30	279	6.0	213.50	227,500	4, 6 pdr	2, 18"	2	62
12	DAVIS	Wolff Zwicker	1896	23.41	22.50	154	5.10	146.00	81,546	3, 1 pdr	3, 18"	2	27
13	FOX	Wolff Zwicker	1896	23.13	23.00	154	5.10	146.00		3, 1 pdr	3, 18"	2	27
14	MORRIS	Herreshoff	1896	24.00	22.50	105	4.1	138.25	144,000	3, 1 pdr	3, 18"	2	21
15	TALBOT	Herreshoff	1896	21.15	20.00	46	3.3	99.50	39,000	1, 1 pdr	2, 18"	2	13
16	GWIN	Herreshoff	1896	20.88	20.00	46	3.3	99.50	39,000	1, 1 pdr	2, 18"	2	13
17	MacKENZIE	Chas Hillman	1896	20.11	20.10	65	4.3	99.25		1, 1 pdr	2, 18"	2	13
18	McKEE	Columbian	1896	19.82	20.00	65	4.3	99.25	45,000	2, 1 pdr	2, 18"		
19	STRINGHAM	Harlam	1897	30.00		340		225.00		4, 5 pdr	2, 18"	3	56
20	GOLDSBOROUGH	Wolff Zwicker	1897	27.40	27.00	255	6.10	198.00		4, 6 pdr	2, 18"	3	61
21	BAILEY	Gas Electric	1897	30.20	30.00	280	4.10	205.00		4, 6 pdr	2, 18"	2	57
22	SOMERS	Schichau	1898	17.05		150		149.25		4, 1 pdr	2, 18"	2	21
23	MANLEY	Yarrow	1898	17.00		30		60.33				1	5
24	BAGLEY	Bath Iron	1898	29.15	29.00	175	4.11	157.00		3, 1 pdr	3, 18"	2	26
25	BARNEY	Bath Iron	1898	29.04	29.00	175	4.11	157.00		3, 1 pdr	3, 18"	2	27
26	BIDDLE	Bath Iron	1898	28.57	28.60	175	4.11	157.00		3, 1 pdr	3, 18"	2	26
27	BLAKELY	Lawley & Sons	1898	25.58	26.00	196	5.11	175.00		3, 1 pdr	3, 18"	2	30
28	DeLONG	Lawley & Sons	1898	25.52	26.00	196	5.11	175.00		3, 1 pdr	3, 18'	2	30
29	NICHOLSON	Lewis Nixon	1898	25.74		218		175.00		3, 1 pdr	3, 18"	2	26
30	O'BRIEN	Lewis Nixon	1898	25.00		220	6.8	175.00		3, 1 pdr	3, 18"	2	26
31	SHUBRICK	Wm. R. Trigg	1898	26.07	25.00	200	5.2	175.00		3, 1 pdr	3, 18"	2	26
32	STOCKTON	Wm. R. Trigg	1898	25.79	25.00	200	5.2	175.00		3, 1 pdr	3, 18"	2	27
33	THORNTON	Wm. R. Trigg	1898	24.88		200		175.00		3, 1 pdr	3, 18"	2	26
34	TINGLEY	Columbian	1898	25.99		165		175.00		3, 1 pdr	3, 18"		
35	WILKES	Gas Electric	1898	25.99	25.99	165	4.8	175.00		3, 1 pdr	3, 18"	2	26

The record of the *Farragut* in attaining the contract speed with only one mistrial is rather remarkable, considering the difficulties experienced with some of the other boats. The *Cushing* and *Dupont* each had three trials and the *Porter* developed defects after preliminary acceptance. The *Ericsson* had several trials, and accidents resulting in the scalding of several men has occurred during the trials of the *Foote* and *Rogers.* The *McKee* was accepted during the recent war without having come up to contract speed. [*Scientific American,* January 28, 1899.]

Torpedo Boat Destroyer No. 14, the Truxtun. *One of the first of the 16 American destroyers authorized in 1898 to combat the growing threat to men-of-war by fleets of deadly torpedo boats was the* Truxtun. *She was 248 feet long, 23 feet 1 1/4 inches beam, and drew 10 feet 11 inches. Her top speed was 30 knots, and her armament included two 3-inch rifles, six 6-pound rifles, and two 18-inch torpedo tubes. The* Truxtun *was laid down on November 13, 1899, at Sparrows Point, Maryland, by the Maryland Steel Company. She was launched on August 15, 1901, and commissioned on September 11, 1902.*

This early torpedo boat destroyer was not a radical design departure from the earlier Herreshoff torpedo boat models of the Talbot type. A close look at the photographs and specifications of the Herreshoff torpedo boats will reveal the slow transition from the fast attack boats to the torpedo boat catcher or the torpedo boat destroyer. (U.S. Navy records.)

Torpedo Boat No. 11, the Farragut. *Launched on July 16, 1898, by the Union Iron Works of San Francisco, the* Farragut *was sponsored by Elizabeth Ashe, Admiral Farragut's niece. The boat was commissioned on June 5, 1899, with Lt. Cmdr. R.F. Nicholson in command. Renamed Coast Torpedo Boat No. 5 on August 1, 1918, she completed her service in the Canal Zone on December 30 that year and arrived at the Mare Island Navy Yard on January 18, 1919. There she was decommissioned on March 13, 1919, and was sold in September 1919.*

Appendix

Rhode Island in the War with Spain

On November 30, 1897, Adjutant Gen. Frederick M. Sackett of Rhode Island sent the first of hundreds of letters and wires concerning the state of readiness of "each company, troop or battery commander, also the commanders of independent organizations," and inquiring what they would do, to prepare for duty in the approaching war "if suddenly called upon to report at Newport with their organizations."

The request for information originated by direction of the commander in chief, Gov. Elisha Dyer. The correspondence and other official records generated over the next 18 months were assembled, published in one volume, and presented by the governor to the General Assembly at its January 1900 session.

In order to document the Bristol connection to the Spanish-American War, the following are excerpted from the collected communications that pertain to Bristol, the Herreshoffs, or torpedo boats.

Naval Reserve Torpedo Company,
Bristol, R.I., March 31, 1898.
Commander W. McCarty Little,
Comdg. Naval Battalion, R.I.
Sir-

I have the honor to report on the steam yachts available for auxiliary work, that, in the opinion of Mr. J.B. Herreshoff, those best suited for such duty are the *Ballymena,* length, 148 feet; beam, 18 feet; speed, 16 knots. Can mount at once four six pounder rapid fire guns, and one or two torpedo tubes. He r owner, Mr. Brown, (while not anxious to sell), is willing to do so if the government desires.

The *Squid,* length, 78 feet; beam, 11 feet was intended as a torpedo boat, primarily. She was built last year, and is some five miles faster than the *Item,* which is not in these waters. Speed, 16 knots, and available at once.

The *Augusta* could be ready in a day and could take our whole battalion if we could have her for ourselves. Length, 94 feet; beam, 12 feet; speed 13 knots. Could mount one pounders and one torpedo tube.

The *Katrina* could also be ready in 24 hours. She is 73 feet long 9 feet beam, and speed of 13 knots. She could take one pounders and [a] torpedo tube.

The *Loon,* 64 feet long, 9 feet beam, and speed of 11 knots is also available. . . .

The *Eugenia* and *Marjorie* were not considered fast enough, nor could the *Nautilus* be for any use requiring speed.

The *Katrina* could be had for $11,000 and the *Squid* for $19,000.

I was unable to get the plans of any except deck and shear of the *Katrina,* though Mr. Herreshoff said he would give plans of any the government would especially desire.

Very respectfully,
W. Fred Williams
Lieut. Comity. Div. 1

Name	Tons	Length	Beam	Depth	Built	Where Built	Date	Owner	Residence
Augusta	38.95	78.4	11.4	7.4	1887	Bristol, RI	1896	J.B. Herreshoff	Bristol
Item	11.45	57.6	8.7	4.4	1896	Bristol, RI	1896	Herreshoff'Mfg.	Bristol
Nautilus	15.55	50.0	10.6	4.8	1898	Boston, MA	1896	H.M. Howe	Bristol
Oberon	16.21	50.8	10.3	4.0	1891	Brooklyn, NY	1896	Herreshoff Mfg.	Bristol
Spalpeen	20.31	66.4	12.5	8.1	1897	Bristol, RI	1897	Robt. M. Riddle	Lansdown, Pa
Eugenia	45.45	70.8	13.6	7.9	1895	Bristol, RI	1895	J.B. Herreshoff	Bristol
Louise	49.8	91.7	14	8.1	1893	Bristol, RI	1893	Herreshoff Mfg	Bristol
Narjorie	40.74	67.0	13.7	8.0	1894	Bristol, RI	1894	A.S. VanWickle	Bristol
Nesham	56.45	97.7	13.7	8.1	1894	Bristol, RI	1896	Herreshoff Mfg.	Bristol
Nina	52.55	92.2	13.7	7.9	1897	Bristol, RI	1897	Herreshoff Mfg.	Bristol

Headquarters R.I. Naval Battalion
Newport, R.I., April 9,1898.
To the Adjutant-General
State of Rhode Island Providence, R.I.
Sir-

In conclusion of my report of March 1st, and in obedience to the order of the A.G.O. of March 28th, I . . . enclose the accompanying lists of vessels of this state from which may be selected such as may be desired by the government for the Mosquito Fleet.

Of the vessels engaged in commerce, or freight, or passenger traffic, the greater part are side wheel steamers. The propellers are small, and hardly come under any of the requirements of blanks 6, 7, or 8, N.W. Photographs of most of the vessels of the Providence, Fall River & Newport Line accompany this report, as well as some of the other vessels mentioned. These will give a very good idea of the types to be found here.

The vessels that would seem to be of use as contemplated in the blanks referred to are the *Nahma,* no where in Newport, but reported about to sail for Scotland; the *Electra,* which is not at present in Rhode Island; and the *Ballymena,* now laid up in Bristol. As small torpedo boats there and also those recommended by Mr. Herreshoff, and spoken of in detail by the annexed report of Lieut. Williams, commanding the Bristol division of this battalion, and which forms part of this report.

Very respectfully, W. McCarty Little
Commander, Commanding R.I. Naval Battalion.

F.P. Garrettson & Co., New York, May 23, 1898.

My Dear Governor [Dyer],
Not long ago, Oliver Belmont offered the U.S. Government a $100,000 torpedo boat which was declined for the reason it was not an unconditional gift. I have reason to believe that if a torpedo boat was built by the Herreshoffs, through popular subscription, and presented by the executive of the state of R.I., that is, yourself, the same would be most gladly accepted. My idea is that the fastest torpedo boat ever built should be constructed by that firm, who are natives of Rhode Island, and [the boat] named after Commodore Perry.[13]

It seems to me that, though this sum is large, there is sufficient patriotism is the state to make it a success. I have personally subscribed $1,000. It seams to me that if prominent men of Providence, and the business men there, would take the matter in hand, through the *Journal, Telegram,* and other papers, and that a concerted movement of the larger towns, including Newport, within a few weeks the sum maybe realized.

Captain McLean of the torpedo station, Lieut. Wm. McCarty Little, Melville Bull, and others are highly in favor of the scheme. I have hardly seen any one as yet, but those whom I have seen, Senators Wetmore and Aldrich, and Mr. Capron.

I am rather sorry to see by the papers this morning, that the affair has leaked out. Your may use this letter as you see fit.

I am, respectfully,
F.P. Garrettson.
New York address, 119 Front St.

State of Rhode Island and Providence Plantations,
Executive Department
Providence, May 26, 1898.
F.P. Garrettson, Esq.,
119 Front Street New York, N.Y.

My Dear Sir,
I am in receipt of your letter of the 23d instant, in relation to the citizens of Rhode Island offering to the United States Government a torpedo boat. I agree with you that the scheme is a truly patriotic one, and I will do whatever I can to aid the cause, although my official duties at this time are so onerous and manifold that I am obliged to devote myself entirely to the interests of the state. I only wish that I had the means at my command to contribute to so worthy a cause.
With best wishes for the success of your project, I am,
Very respectfully,
Elisha Dyer.

About the Author

A native of Rhode Island, Richard V. Simpson is a contributing editor for *Antiques & Collecting Magazine.* Some 50 of his articles on the subjects of antique glass, china, and art pottery have appeared in the magazine since 1985. Schooled in the graphic arts, Simpson is a retired visual information specialist from the Naval Undersea Warfare Center (NUWC) in Newport, Rhode Island. He is also a professional fine art painter whose works were exhibited widely in southeastern New England competitions during the 1960s and 1970s. He is a recipient of the Nerone Award from the Bristol Art Museum and the Aldrich Prize of the Providence Art Club.

His first book, *Independence Day: How the Day is Celebrated in Bristol, Rhode Island* (1989), documents the nation's oldest Fourth of July celebration, beginning in 1785. Simpson served for many years as a member of the Bristol Fourth of July Celebration Committee, serving as parade float judge, member of the executive board and, at various times, chairman of several different celebration subcommittees. He became committee historian when the post was established, serving in that capacity from 1971 to 1976. His continued in-depth research of the annual parade, along with several continuing volunteer roles with the annual Independence Day celebration has earned him the title of Bristol's *de facto* Fourth of July historian. In 1994, he was honored by the Town of Bristol by being appointed Patriotic Speaker of the Day for the Fourth of July patriotic exercises—a position second only to that of the grand marshal of the parade. He was interviewed as subject matter expert for an article in *Yankee* magazine (July 1989) and acted as consultant for the parade sequence in the movie *Mr. North.*

His interest in Rhode Island history, art, and antiques has led to many articles in the *Bristol Phoenix, Providence Journal,* and *Newtown Bee.* From 1984 until retirement in early 1996, he was publication designer and editorial writer for *Sting,* a local bimonthly union newsletter. He is currently working on a companion volume to *Independence Day* called *The Day That We Celebrate,* which further documents Bristol's Fourth of July history. In 1994, his history of St. Mary's Church, *Old Mother Church in Bristol, Rhode Island,* was published by the Taylor Publishing Company. His photographic history *Bristol, Rhode Island* was published in March 1996 by Arcadia Publishing. Three additional town biographies—Portsmouth, Rhode Island, and two volumes titled *Tiverton and Little Compton, Rhode Island*—were published in 1996 and 1997. A second volume of Bristol photographic history and a photographic history of the America's Cup yacht races were published by Arcadia Publishing in 1998 and 1999, respectively.

Endnotes

In the interest of the reader, sources and references have been incorporated in brief format generally throughout the text. Also, because much of the narrative is based upon accounts in 19th-century newspapers, periodicals, and official naval records, an effort has been made to keep the text relatively free of intrusive referencing. Many historical statistics are available in the Naval War College Archives and in technical documents issued by the modern successor establishments of the Naval Torpedo Station at Newport.

1. An editorial in the *Bristol Phoenix* on October 21, 1893, noted: "The *Vigilant*'s success is Bristol's . . . for this is the birthplace of the yacht that outsails the world and brings fame to her designers. 'Nat Herreshoff won't give a fellow a chance to win' was the disgusted comment of one of Capt. Nat's old-time adversaries." This editorial shows the prominence had at the onset by the Rhode Island boatbuilder:

> Our amiable and sportsman like visitor Lord Dunraven probably feels about that way himself. New York is boasting now of her first victory in the international contest since *Genesia* came over. For it was a Boston boat that beat *Genesia* and a Boston boat that beat *Thistle*. But in the former competitions to select a defender for the America's Cup, Boston's *Volunteer* had no competitor to meet *Thistle*. The New York boats were built in New York.
>
> This year New York came to Bristol for a boat and the result was *Vigilant* and *Colonia,* two of the dandiest flyers that the world has ever known. The *Phoenix* rises to remark that it is proud of the fact that it hails from the same town as Nat Herreshoff!

2. Documents relating to torpedo history and development issued by the former Naval Underwater Systems Center provide background on the early history, relevant parts of which may be found, for example, in John Merrill and Lionel Wyld, *Meeting the Submarine Challenge: A Short History of the Naval Underwater Systems Center, Newport:* United States Government Printing Office, 1997.

3. The *Bristol Phoenix*, "The Navy in Newport." For further source material on Goat Island, see documents in the Naval War College Archives.

4. Refer to the charts in chapters 11 and 12 for these and other statistics on the various vessels.

5. From the *Frank Leslie Illustrated Newspaper* of June 20, 1885, in an article entitled "The Swift *Stiletto:* An Eye-witness Account of the Boat's Hudson River Races."

6. As indicated in the text, several contemporary accounts in the press provided source material for this chapter—for example, this from the *Bristol Phoenix* of January 1893:

> An order was received by the Herreshoff Manufacturing Co., of this town, last week, from the Assistant Secretary of the Navy, Mr. Soley, for a steam launch twenty-eight feet in length, to be used at the Massachusetts Nautical Training School in connection with the Training Ship *Enterprise.* The government has experimented a great deal with steam launches but none have stood the test as well as those made by the Herreshoffs.

7. See L. Francis Herreshoff's *Captain Nat Herreshoff: The Wizard of Bristol* (1953).

8. Armstrong, G.E. *Torpedoes & Torpedo-Vessels.* Royal Navy handbook. George Bell and Sons, 1889.

9. Young, James Rankin. *Reminiscences and Thrilling Stories of the War.* Philadelphia: J.H. Moore Company, 1899.

10. Daniels, Josephus. *The First Fallen Hero*. Norfolk, Virginia: S.W. Bowman, 1898.

11. Mead, Lt. Ernest E. "The Rescue of the Winslow." *Harper's Monthly,* 1898–1899.

12. Young. *Reminiscences.*

13. Commo. Oliver Hazard Perry, a native Rhode Islander (Newport), was the first commander of the U.S. Navy. Perry distinguished himself at the Battle of Lake Erie in September 1813.

Index

The following is a partial listing of terms found in this volume.